Copyright 2022 Patricia Giglio
All Rights Reserved

Cover Image: Andover Haunted House
Photo Credit: Patricia Giglio

ISBN: 979-8-218-03870-0

Notice: The information in the book is true and complete to the best of my knowledge. It is offered without guarantee on the part of the author. The author disclaims all liability in connection with the use of this book.

All rights reserved. No part of this book may be reproduced or transmitted in any form whatsoever without prior written permission from the author except in the case of brief quotations embodied in critical articles and reviews.

This book is dedicated to my husband Steve who has always been by biggest fan and cheering section. To my children, Liesl and Karl, for loving their mom. To my dear friends, Sally and Karen, who are great partners in crime and adventure. To my friend Cheryl who puts up with my craziness. To my soul sister Joanie. And my friends and family, both blood and not, who encourage me and support my "habit."

A Woman Scorn

The sleepy village of Aurora is nestled along the eastern shore of Cayuga Lake. The history of Aurora was shaped by the Morgan Family, who were businessmen and investors in some of the most important local and state ventures in history, as well as members of "secret societies," like the freemasons.

Colonel Edwin Barber Morgan had perhaps the biggest influence on Aurora's history than any other member of his family. Edwin moved to Aurora from New York City when he was just a baby. He would become the original investor of the New York Times and a US House Representative. In 1833 Edwin built the Aurora House, or as villagers called it "Morgan's Brick Tavern", which was used as a meeting house for village officials. The Aurora House became a stagecoach stop for weary, dusty travelers. Great food and drink were served, and the accommodations offered were comfortable, and the Aurora House soon became a famous establishment along the well-worn route. When the Cayuga-Seneca Canal opened to traffic, the tavern served those travelers as well.

Etching of the Aurora Inn

Morgan ran the Aurora House until the 1840s when he sold it to William D. Eagles. Though William and his family never lived in the Aurora House; his uncle, John Eagles, managed the property for him. John, who was quite an interesting character who at one time ran a traveling circus with a troupe of men, seventy horses and two elephants.

The Morgan family would again regain control of the property when Edwin's brother Henry, not Captain Henry Morgan of rum fame, acquired it. When Henry died on May 11, 1887, the family decided to sell the property to Coral Smith.

It is at this point that the connection between the Aurora House and Wells College was formed.

Fire destroyed the main building at Wells College in 1888, which caused more excitement in one night than the village had seen in its entire history. Most of the students at the all-women college were displaced. The college contracted with the Aurora House to be used as student dorms until the new dorm house was finished in 1890. The girls displaced by the fire affectionately nicknamed the Aurora House the Wayside Inn, a name stuck for years.

Wells College had not forgot how the Aurora House came to their aid and was able to return the favor decades later. Aurora's tiny business district was rocked by fire in February 1919. The flames got closer to the Aurora House, and when the news of the fire reached KD MacMillan, the president of Wells College, he sprung to action and raced to the inn. MacMillan laid on the roof and extinguished the flames that licked at the cornice the brick building and continued to protect it until the threat was over.

After several ownership changes, RL Zabriskie, the final owner, gave the Aurora House to Wells College on March 30, 1943. In 1948, it would officially become the Aurora Inn. After just over a century of being a mainstay in Aurora, the inn fell in hard times and closed its doors in the 1970s. Like so many buildings like it, the inn fell into a sad state of disrepair and remained empty for almost 30 years. In 2003 the new owners undertook a major renovation project, and it became the luxurious inn it is today.

Henry Wells was the best friend of Colonel Edwin Barber Morgan. Like Morgan, he came to Aurora from New York City with his family. Wells was a very successful businessman who merged his company American Express with Merchant Union Express Company in Aurora forming the Wells, Fargo & Co. in 1868.

Also in 1868, Henry Wells opened the Wells Seminary, now Wells College, an all-women college. Wells and his wife Mary were very involved in the college's daily business, right down to the most mundane tasks. On Friday nights, students were often invited to dine with the Wells at their home, Glen Park. The couple were a beloved part of the girls' collegiate experience. While Henry was traveling abroad in Glasgow, Scotland he became ill and passed away 2 days shy of his 73rd birthday. His body was brought back to Aurora and laid to rest at Oak Glen Cemetery. Although he had achieved tremendous success throughout his lifetime, he left behind some financial problem that his wife and family could not clear up. Glen Park went into foreclosure and Mary was forced to leave the home that she loved and shared with Henry. The Wells College Alumni Association bought the house in 1905. Mary Wells was very happy to know that Glen Park would become a part of the college that had become such a huge part of their lives.

Glen Park, Home of Henry and Mary Wells. The bridge in front is where the spirit of the jealous wife is seen.

Both the Aurora Inn and Wells College have a great history that is recorded in many books written about the village. But those books fail to mention the tales of moments in history that are stamped into the fabric of time and still roam the college halls and plush lawns of the inn.

During the 1919 fire almost all of Aurora's downtown area was reduced to ashes when homes and businesses were destroyed. One structure that fell victim to the flames was an old building along the lakeshore near the Aurora Inn. A legend passed down through the generations was that there were three people trapped inside the burning structure, two men and a woman. The men have been witnessed by many over the years as apparitions pacing along the lake near where the ruins of the building sit in the village park. The woman, who has been dubbed the Lady in White, makes her appearance inside the Aurora Inn gliding through the lobby and some of the guest rooms.

Wells College has more than its fair share of ghost stores and has the privilege of being called the most haunted college campus in the United States.

The Pettibone House was built by George Pettibone in 1857. Pettibone was rumored to be a gambler and major player in the New York City financial scene. It was also whispered that he was in a very rocky and tumultuous marriage. After George's death the Pettibone House became part of the college campus as an upperclassmen dormitory at the turn of the twentieth century. During one spring semester in the early 1900s, friends Ann and Mary were unpacking their suitcases after returning from spring break. While the roommates chatted, they were joined by a friend named Edith. Edith did not seem to act like her normal cheerful self, in fact she was very quiet and sad. Concerned, the girls asked Edith what was wrong, and she told them that she was worried about losing touch with them after graduation. They hugged their friend and told her she was just being silly. Edith walked out of the room and told them she wanted to go see Carol and would be back. When Edith did not return, they went looking for her. Ann and Mary ran into Carol, who said she had not seen her. Moments later, the three girls were called to the Dean's office and were told that Edith had been killed in a car accident on the way back to the college, she never made it to campus.

During the first decade of the twentieth century the country was gripped by a deadly influenza epidemic. Every corner of this great nation was affected, including Wells College. Students began to become ill, and the fourth floor of the main building was turned into a makeshift hospital. All the nurses on staff could do was keep the sick comfortable and pray for their recovery. Unfortunately, some of them died from the illness. Not being a proper hospital made storing the bodies of the dead difficult and they were placed in rooms until their families could make funeral arrangements. The door to one of the rooms was painted red to distinguish it from the others, so that no one would accidentally stumble into their resting place. After the epidemic was over and all the bodies had been claimed, the fourth floor was once again used as dormitory. The red door was painted over again and again. No matter how much paint was applied, the red would always bleed through as a gruesome reminder of the tragic events. The red door, however, is not the only reminder of the influenza epidemic. Some students housed on the fourth floor have said that they have awaken in the middle of the night to see an apparition of a nurse place an icy hand on their forehead, and then disappear before their eyes.

Some of the stories are wrought with jealousy and secret love affairs. Such is the case of the Pettibone House. The original affair happened before the college bought it. There was a man in the village that was in a torrid love affair with a young woman boarder at the Pettibone House. His wife suspected that she had been cheated on and followed him as he sneaked out one night. The wife came across her husband's mistress on the bridge between Glen Park and the Pettibone House. She reached inside her coat, pulled out a knife and stabbed the poor woman to death. Years after the murder, a light on the bridge will go off and the ghost of the jealous wife can be seen pulling the knife from her coat.

At the Crossroads

If you look behind the commercial buildings in Victor near East View Mall, there are a few buildings that date back to the mid-19th century. They are the remnants of Valentown, a community that had once offered great promise to those who lived there. Ichabod Town built a log cabin near the intersection of three Indians trails in 1809. It was the beginning of a small village that thrived for decades with a cooper shop, blacksmith shop, trading post and school. Its location was important during the infancy of our growing nation. During the War of 1812, American troops would regularly camp in the square, and it would remain a gathering place until the turn of the 20th century.

Valentown, a four-story community and commercial center built by Levi Valentine in 1879.

The expansion of the railroad was once a guarantee of growth and prosperity for any town or village across the nation. When Levi Valentine, Ichabod's grandson, heard that the Pittsburgh, Shawmut & Northern Railroad had planned to lay their new tracks through the village, a light bulb lit up in his head and in 1879 Valentown was founded. He had a plan to capitalize on that piece of news.

Levi built a four-story that would serve as a community hall and commercial center. It was first indoor shopping center in the area. The building was designed to service the needs of the citizens. The banked basement had a horse stable and blacksmith shop. On the first floor there was a general store, bakery, harness shop, a cobbler, and a large meeting room. The second floor housed a music school, a railroad and telegraph office, as well as meeting rooms for the Grange and the Independent Order of Good Templar. The massive building was topped with a grand ballroom where dances and other social gatherings were held.

Valentown saw great success that brought people from all over the countryside. However, the dreams that Valentown had of wealth and prosperity were soon dashed when they received word that the railroad had gone bankrupt before the tracks reached them. Although it was able to survive for several years, Valentown would eventually be abandoned.

The massive building fell into a horrible state of disrepair, to the point that the owners at one time decided to demolish it for salvage. Before it could be dismantled, Sheldon Fisher and his wife purchased it and the Ichabod Town homestead in 1940. Fisher had a great love for history and began to restore the great hall. After the massive restoration was complete, he opened a museum that he called the "Ghost City of Valentown" and founded the Victor Historical Society. The museum is filled with more than 35,000 artifacts that include human bones found in a box after Fisher's death in 2002. Four years before his death, the museum became part of the historical society, and they have been the caretakers of its past ever since.

With a written history of more than two hundred years and stories that have been passed down even farther back, it is not hard to see why there are a multitude of ghosts that wander the grounds. Every floor of the Valentown museum seems to have a ghost story, or two, associated with it. But why wouldn't it, Valentown itself is nothing but a ghost town.

Shortly after the hall opened there was a terrible wagon accident along the road to Valentown. A little girl by the name of Sarah was thrown from the wagon and she was carried into the stable while awaiting a doctor to tend to her. She died within minutes. An apparition of a girl about 8-years old, the same age Sarah was when she died, has been seen walking around the basement. She seems to be interested in what people visiting the museum are doing. If there is a child in the group, it is said that she will follow them as if asking them to play.

Though all the spiritual activity in the basement cannot be attributed to one little girl. Tools moved on their own and the sounds of shuffling feet are heard in dark corners. The human bones mentioned before were found in a box in the basement, their identity remains a mystery. Tucked away in an old stable stall is an ambulance wagon used during the American Revolution. Could this interesting artifact be responsible for some of the activity?

1770s wagon used during the American Revolution.

Of all the shops on the first floor, the most popular was the bakery, filled with decadent treats and breads. Visitors at Valentown can smell the aroma of fresh baked breads and pies. But it is not only the curious visitors that have been seen coming in and out of the shop's door. Shadows move about the bakery as if trying to decide which delicious treat to try. As you take in the wonderful store front displays, be careful not to step on the phantom cat that might curl itself around your feet.

The atmosphere of the second floor is quieter and more solemn, compared to the floor of shops, especially around the exhibits in the military room that pay homage to those who served this great country as far back as the American Revolution. A ghostly figure of a soldier is said to stand in a silent vigil over the memory of fallen brothers. Also in the same room, a magazine's pages flip inside a locked case. But not all the ghostly activity comes from the military room. Across the hall, the music room is filled with a variety of musical instruments, including a piano and Victrola. Unseen hands play phantom symphonies on the piano's keys and set a record of their favorite composer on the Victrola.

Ballroom/community gathering place located on the top floor of the Valentown building.

During the day the grand ballroom is full of life and light, the walls lined with tall windows. But as darkness falls, shadows begin to play at the top of the staircase. They could be the product of a legend that has been passed down through the generations that tells of a crime of passion that happened more than a century ago. At a quadrille dance, a popular social event in the 19th century, a local military band played while a girl and boy danced. The boy was not her betrothed and when the girl's fiancé walked into the room, he flew into a jealous rage, pulled out his revolver and shot her dance partner dead. Soft musical notes and lemon verbena waft through the air just before the mood takes a dark turn.

Anyone can visit the museum at the corner of High Street and Valentown Road during the day. Don't tarry too long after the sun starts to sink because the night belongs to the past.

Awaiting the Curtain Call

Although the first settlers came to the shores of the crooked lake in 1799, Penn Yan was not officially founded until 1833. When most people think of Penn Yan, they see a peaceful and simple countryside village with farms of the Amish dotting the rolling hills. However, in the early 1800s the village was much different. Like all "frontier" communities on the western edge of the new nation, it was a wild and sometimes violent place to live.

As the 19th century progressed, the citizens of this booming village grew more refined. Sure, Penn Yan had its fair share of saloons that lined the dirt Main Street, but by the turn of the twentieth century there were theaters and opera houses peppered in between. The majestic Sampson Theatre was one of the establishments that brought culture to the frontier. Parts of the theater's past still clings to the structure. To understand why ghosts lurk in the dark auditorium, we must understand the history of not only the building, but the land that it sits on.

Jacob Street, which is now East Elm, is in the heart of the historic district and is one of the original streets in Penn Yan. Before 1872 there were no complete records and map of the town. So, the story of the Sampson Theatre and the lot that it claimed on Jacob Street begins there.

In April 1872 a fire was sparked from the Commercial Iron Works' chimney and caught the roof on fire. Fires were common in the mid-19th century and after continuously rebuilding from fire after fire, the town had come up with an action plan to keep the flames down. Whenever a spark would ignite the roof, a man would walk across a wooden plank with a bucket of water and douse the flames. However, on this day, the wooden plank was broken, and the man couldn't cross in to extinguish the flames before the fire got out of control. Within in three hours every building on the block was destroyed. It was believed that one man had perished in the fire, though a body was never recovered. The victim was a Civil War veteran named Martin Hope who served with the Blue Boys of Yates County. Could he have died on the site of the Sampson Theatre?

After the fire, the buildings popped up along Jacob Street, except on the lot that Eli Sheldon owned, which stayed empty until 1877 when the Wagener Mansion was moved there. The mansion was originally built in 1816 by Abraham Wagener, first as the family home and then a hotel. It was also rumored to have been a stop on the Underground Railroad. Three years after it was moved to its new location, the Wagener Mansion met the same fate that many other buildings did and was destroyed by a fire in March 1880. The building was not rebuilt, and the lot remained empty for another three decades.

Dr. Frank S. Sampson decided to build a theatre in 1910. The prominent physician chose the empty lot on Jacob Street for the first concrete and brick, fire-proof theatre that would be known as the Sampson Theatre. For the theatre to open, Dr. Sampson put a stipulation in the contract that at least 500 tickets needed to be sold for opening night. To the surprise of many, opening night was sold-out and everyone was treated to a fantastic experience. The inside of the theatre was beautiful, with a hand-painted stage curtain with the image of Esperanza Mansion which had been donated by Wendell Bush.

Postcard from 1922 of the Sampson Theatre in Penn Yan.

For the ten years that Dr. Sampson owned the theatre, it was very successful. After he sold it, movie houses became all the rage, and it could no longer compete with the Elm Theatre that was just down the street. In 1928, the Sampson Theatre closed its doors and

Henry Morse converted it into an indoor miniature golf course. The building then became an automobile garage and showroom, and a tire warehouse.

In 2004 the Pennsylvania Yankee Theatre Company bought the aging building and began restoring it to its former glory. As the stage that had been hidden for decades was brough back to life, so were that ghosts that resided with the walls. Their stories had waited a long time to be told. The most prominent ghost in the theatre is that of Eunice Frame, the pianist from the Sampson Theatre. Miss Frame had a passion for music and not only played at the theatre, but also was the organist at the First Methodist Church in Penn Yan. Even though throughout the history of the theatre there were many people worked there, the spirits that roam the aisles and sit in the balcony could be from the past long before the first walls were poured.

Bricks and Stones, Ghosts and Spirits

Geneva was originally the Seneca village of Kanadasaga. During the British occupation of the colonies, the Seneca tribes were strong allies of the British army and orchestrated brutal attacks on the defenseless settlers. Through this alliance the Senecas allowed Kanadasaga to be used as British fortification. After a hard-fought victory in the American Revolution, General George Washington ordered the destruction of all the Indians villages that sided with the enemy. Major General John Sullivan was given the task of exacting the revenge of a battered nation. In 1779 Sullivan and his army leveled the village of Kanadasaga and the British fort. Even though the Seneca fought side by side with Britain against the colonists, the royal crown did not offer the same support when Sullivan's army came sweeping through. Those who had survived the attack by the army were forced to move and the village was abandoned and left in ruins for over a decade. Like other areas of the state, it wasn't long before the new frontier opened, and the settlers began to pour in.

Lands agents for Gorham and Phelps, along with a small group of families arrived in Geneva in 1793. The streets were mapped out and the village's population soon exploded. Businesses filled Castle and Seneca Streets. Houses lined the lengths of Main and Pultney. Mills and other forms of industry took hold of the property along the lakeshore to the north of the village and mansions built by their owners took over the southern edge.

When the Cayuga-Seneca Canal opened in 1825, Geneva had a successful waterfront where businesses continued to grow and flourish. The first railroad was completed in 1841 that connected Auburn to Rochester and pushed commerce to the rails and away from the water. Geneva adapted well to the new steam powered giants that moved progress along. Until the turn of the 20th century, Geneva's industrial assets multiplied by leaps and bounds. It would then become a center of culture and enlightenment. With Geneva's history spanning over two hundred years, some of her greatest structures cling to pieces of the past.

The Geneva Theatre, or the Smith Opera House, located on Seneca Street between Main and Exchange is one of the oldest operating opera houses in the United States. The façade of this beautiful 1894 stone building has two medallions, one of famed playwright William Shakespeare and the other is Edwin Booth. Booth was hands down the most popular stage actor in the 1800s, and the brother of Lincoln's assassin John Wilkes Booth.

An image of the inside of the Smith Opera House in 1894.

Geneva had become a haven for contemporary thinkers; feminists, writers and authors flocked to the lakeside town, and with them they brought a need for cultural outlets. For a short time, the village had two opera houses: the Linden and the Geneva Theatre. Sadly, the Linden was destroyed by fire just two months after the Geneva opened and ten years later it almost succumbed to the same fate. On March 18, 1904, the Smith Block was ravaged by a devasting fire that started in the building block next to it. The skill and tenacity of the local fireman saved the flames from jumping the small alley and lighting up the theatre. It would be progress and not fire that would be the biggest threat to its survival.

By the 1920s, the opera house could not compete with the movie houses that popped up and it fell into a state of disrepair. A local entrepreneur saw potential in this tarnished jewel and in 1929 renovated it into a grand movie palace that attracted all the glamorous celebrities of the day.

The purpose (and name) of the Smith Opera House changed throughout the years. Here it was called the Geneva.

The misty form of a woman is known to roam the halls and sit in the balcony of this historic monument. No one knows who the mysterious spirit is. Is she a fallen star of the stage waiting for her eternal curtain call? Or has her love of the silver screen kept her forever featured in her own silent film?

In the paranormal field, we all too often run into a situation where rumors surround a building but there are very few details to shed light on the mystery. As is the case of the Dove Building, built around 1886 by William Dove who came to Geneva from Canandaigua with his wife, Florence, and their son Arthur. Dove was originally a farmer, but he soon became disenchanted with that life and moved to the seashore to pursue his dream of being a lobsterman. Frustrated with her husband's choices, Florence chose to stay on the family farm. The Dove men were dreamers. And although William risked it all the follow his dream to the coast, he did not approve of Arthur's aspiration to be an artist. Arthur went against his parent's wishes and became one of America's first abstract painters.

Looking at the building from the sidewalk, the stone façade gives an awesome aura of strength. The four-story building served many purposes over the years. The basement once housed a fish market and other odd shops. It was also rumored that during epidemics and times of tragedy, the basement was used as a makeshift morgue to store bodies. The first floor always served as a tavern or saloon. And the second floor had several small tenement apartments. In 1913, a small apartment had an accidental fire that was set by one of the four children that lived there. The charred exposed bricks serve as a reminder of the tragedy that can happen when children are left to their own devices. When I visited the building in 2012, all the apartments had been stripped down except for a few oddly placed claw foot tubs. A wide curved, almost grand, staircase leads from the second floor to a loft with a twelve-foot ceiling and inlaid tiles. In the center of the room was a solitary tub.

The Dove Block in the early 1900s.

The apartments had not been rented for years, the last tenant on the first floor of the Dove Block was a restaurant. The restaurant had been very successful, so it was a surprise when it suddenly closed in 2004. The owners locked the doors and left their personal belongings in the office and basement. After that, the building sat empty for years...or has it? Do spirits of the dead belly up to the bar for a stiff drink? Or could the bitter ghost of Florence Dove be trying to hold onto her dignity in the afterlife?

According to those who last worked in the building, they regularly experienced the unexplained. Voices and music have been heard coming from behind doors that were locked, and phantom boot heels clicked on the hardwood floors. Both employees and patrons reported being pinched, scratched, and hit. The basement was the one place that the staff never wanted to go. As soon as the bottom step of the basement stairs was reached, the atmosphere quickly changed. It felt as if they were not alone, an unseen entity followed them through the shadows and watched their every move. One of the owners went a step further and claimed to have been locked in the walk-in basement freezer when no one else was in the building. Could that have been the straw that broke the camel's back and gave them no other choice than to walk away?

Not all of Geneva's haunted locations are still standing. When Captain Charles Williamson came to America in 1781, he was a ranking member of the British military. Upon his arrival in Boston, Williamson expected to be greeted by Lord Cornwallis, instead he found himself face to face with the U.S. Navy. He and his men were taken prisoner and held aboard the ship *Marquis* just outside of Salem, Massachusetts. Being unhappy with his military career serving the British Crown, Williamson sold his commission and gained his freedom. Instead of being sent on to a prison run by the rebelling colonists, he was welcomed with open arms into the home of Ebenezer Newell in Brookfield, Massachusetts and he later married Newell's daughter Abigail. When the war ended Williamson returned to England with his wife, but their stay was short lived.

On January 9, 1792, Charles Williamson became a U.S. citizen in a Philadelphia court and was ready to begin his career as a land agent for Gorham and Phelps. Williamson mapped many of the settlements in the wilds of Western New York; including Lyons, Sodus, Bath and of course Geneva. In Geneva, he helped plan the principal streets and erected several ley buildings in the town's history. Some of the buildings are still used today, such as the Williamson Hotel which is now the Pultney Apartments.

Williamson was also credited with the construction of what would be the first haunted house in Geneva, Mile Point House which once stood at the southern end of Main Street. The street had been laid out in such a way that each house was built on the west side of the road with a commanding view of Seneca Lake. Poplar trees lined both sides of the street and it curved inland as it reached the end. Williamson felt that his stature in the community should be rewarded with the best lakeside view. In 1796, he started to build a beautiful brick mansion, which he called Mile Point House, that was the only house that was between the street and the lake, he truly had an unobstructed view of the water. Mile Point House was intended to be the grandest of all houses, but it was never finished. For reasons unknown, the very sight of the house brought people an extreme feeling of terror and it quickly gained the reputation of being haunted. It remains a mystery to this day as to why. Around 1830 Mile Point House was demolished and no trace of the building was left, except for a few poplar trees that had offered a spectacular view of an empty lot. The Houghton House, which is part of Hobart and William Smith Colleges, is built on the site of Mile Point House.

I have no doubt that dozens more buildings in Geneva have spirits wandering through them. As you walk down Main Street listen carefully as the houses scream to you that they have a story to tell. Will you take a step or two closer to hear what they have to say?

Checked Out

When the town of Naples was established in 1789 on the southern shore of Canandaigua Lake, the land was deemed worthless because of its hilly topography. It was later discovered that despite its rolling landscape, the soil was perfect for the cultivation of grapes. Since 1961, people from all over the world come to the Finger Lakes region to sample the grapes and wine produced here and visit the annual Naples Grape Festival.

Not only could Naples boast about their famous grape pies, but the town was also home to the "finest brick hotel in Ontario County." The largest brick structure in the area was built in 1895 with walls that were five bricks deep, a building that was built to last. Jeff R. Brown's hotel offered room and board with fine dining for the travelers, as well as a stable and feed for their horses. As horses were replaced by cars, people continued travel to the Naples Hotel for a delicious meal and stay the night.

The Naples Hotel at the turn of the 20th century.

Throughout the twentieth century, the Naples Hotel has had many famous guests, some looked for a hidden elegant place to relax while others worked to further their political careers. Robert

Kennedy, then US Attorney General, gave a moving speech on the hotel's front porch just a month before his assassination. Other celebrity guests include radio personality Paul Harvey.

In the Naples Hotel's 127-year history, there is only one supposed death. According to local legend, a traveling salesman arrived at the hotel in the 1930s and was found hanging in his third-floor room, his death an apparent suicide. Could he have been distraught by his financial ruin amid the Great Depression?

The hotel changed ownership several times since its construction. With most historic properties that are for sale, the price to own it isn't always measured in dollars. A prospective buyer leased the hotel and soon after began to experience strange things. The incidents began to take a toll on him mentally and emotionally, slowly driving him insane. The man would be seen for the last time running from the Naples Hotel, his life in ruins.

Could the ghost in the Naples Hotel be the mysterious stranger who ended his life at the end of a rope. Or perhaps it is the spirit of Jeff Brown keeping a close watch on the "finest hotel" that he built from the ground up.

Curious Little Louis

The Erie Canal brought wealth and prosperity to the village of Brockport. Houses and businesses seemed to pop up overnight. Ansel Chappell, a business partner of William Seymour and Dayton Manning in the Globe Iron Works, built his home on State Street in 1855. The two-story brick home was one of the finer, more modest homes in the village. Some of its original features remain after 167 years – the rooftop cupola and elegant curved staircase. In the basement, remnants of the Dutch oven and flame-kissed walls are still set in the stone foundation.

Even though the Chappell family was well-respected, they were not immune to scandal. Thomas Chappell, Ansel's son, was arrested for his role in one of the biggest banking frauds of the time. He sold bogus checks written against his father's account to the sum of thousands of dollars. This exploded into what would be known as the "Canton Bank Scandal." The Chappell family would lose their home as a result.

The old Fowler Funeral Home.

On a village of Brockport map dated 1872, George R. Ward is listed as the owner. Ward was a grocer on Main Street, as well as the proprietor of the Ward Opera Block. He was a respected, hard-working man, and his wife Marion Root was loved by all. After George passed away in 1889, she married Henry Dewey who took her heart and moved into her home. Dewey was, among other things, a village justice of the peace. You can only imagine how many love-struck couples knocked on the door and asked to be married in the dark of the night. Or the shotgun weddings that took place in the front parlor. Many happy moments filled the rooms before the tragic ones associated with one of the future owners. Henry Dewey passed away in 1917, Marion followed him into death 4 years later.

In the 1940s, Alonso Fowler bought the brick home with the intention to turn it into a funeral home, for fifty years it would be the Fowler Funeral Home. It would eventually move to its present location on West Avenue.

The basement kitchen was replaced by a morgue and laboratory space. The parlor where secret elopements took place became viewing rooms that would be filled with sadness.

The Fowler family were the most notable owners of 52 State Street, even though they never lived there. Alonso Fowler was the son of Arthur and Adele, as well as the husband of Olive Daily. Originally Alonso was part owner of the Daily-Fowler Funeral Home on Main Street. Before Alonso was drafted into the military to serve his country in World War I, Austen Daily sold his interest in the funeral home to Alonso, who had not only been his business partner, but was also his son-in-law. And thus began a family business. Alonso's son Keith joined the family business in 1932 followed by Vincent in the 1950s. Cortlandt, Vincent's son, is now in charge of the business…carrying on a 125-year-old legacy.

Many people have passed through this old building on their way to eternal rest. Some never left and continue to call the building home, a curious little boy, a loving mother, and a grumpy old man.

In canal town accidental drownings were commonplace, especially those that involved children and a child's death was more tragic than any other. Little Louis was a darling three-year-old boy with a head filled with black curls and big green eyes. Like most small children, Louis was full of mischief and curiosity. He was not one to hang on the apron strings of his mother, perhaps if he did this story would have a much different ending. Louis' mother had been widowed for less than a year and he was the only link to her dead husband.

Louis had the habit of wandering from home at all hours of the day and night, often being led home by a neighbor's hand. One morning in the wee hours, while his mother slept, Louis stood upon a chair and unlocked the front door. He was eager to get an early start to explore the world outside. Barefoot and in his nightshirt, he walked out into the dark.

The rising sun woke his mother. As she got ready for the day, she saw the chair and the front door ajar. She began to frantically look throughout the house for little Louis, but in her heart, she knew he would not be found there.

She ran outside and called his name. Instinct led her to the canal and to her horror a barge man pulled something from the water. With his back to her, she saw his shoulders shake as he sobbed. In his arms was the lifeless body of curious little Louis.

Louis' mother was overcome with grief. His little body was taken to the funeral home and laid out for burial. Curiosity may have gotten to best of Louis in life, but it would not stop him in death. In the early hours, while the building is still, the sound of tiny footsteps can be heard in the hall of the old funeral home, followed by that of a chair being dragged and the click of the tumbler lock as it is turned.

The original oak coffin elevator rests in the shaft in the basement ready to take the next body up to one of the viewing rooms on the first floor. How many times have you heard "if these walls could talk..." when you visit an old building? Sometimes the walls of this old funeral home do talk, especially those behind the heavy wooden elevator doors. Most of the voices heard coming from the shaft are confused utterances begging to be let out, unaware that they have passed on. Voices from beyond the grave aren't the only spirit activities associated with the elevator shaft.

Inside the elevator shaft, there are double doors at the first floor for the coffin to be brought through and a single man door at the second floor. There is, however, no opening for that door on the outside of the shaft, it has been completely sealed shut. Traditionally doors were sealed shut to keep spirits from entering through them. How many spirits thought that they could escape the afterlife through that door and be reunited with their loved ones?

Often the spirits that roam the halls of a building, do not know that they have died. This is the case of a woman that is in search of her baby. The woman was in her fourth month of pregnancy when she became deathly ill and she lost her unborn child shortly before she died in a feverish fit. The woman's body was brought to the funeral home to be prepared for burial. Not long after her burial, her spirit came back looking for her baby, unaware that they were both dead. Footsteps begin on the first floor, then run up the stairs through the second-floor rooms, to the cupola and back down again. The frantic mother searches every inch of the house for her precious baby, the child she will never find.

Each body that came to the old Fowler Funeral Home had story to tell, a life that was lived. There were other stories of death that are linked to workers at the Fowler and Daily-Fowler Funeral Homes.

In 1892 Brockport was victim to a string of fires that had been labeled as arson. The prime suspect was Frank Griffin, an employee of the Daily-Fowler Funeral Home. He cared for their horses and drove the horse-drawn hearse. Though Griffin was never convicted of arson, the rumors followed him until his death in 1900. At the age of 32, Frank Griffin was kicked by one of the horses he cared for and died from his injuries. He was buried in an unmarked grave at High Street Cemetery.

Benjamin Gleason also worked at the funeral home as a mortician. He also invented the first mortuary cooling table. The table had a thin metal top with a beautifully ornate punched design. Ice was put under the table to keep the body cool and slow the decomposition process during the viewings. What went through the factory employees mind as they made the table that they would be placed upon after their life ended.

Curse in the Wood

Construction on the Ithaca Automobile Sales and Service Building began in the summer of 1915, a building that would later be incorporated into the State Theatre. As work crews excavated the former Wool Bakery site for the cellar of the new dealership, they made a grisly discovery. It would be big news in the small Tompkins County city, and an article appeared in the August 25th edition of the Ithaca Journal. *"...workmen today unearthed a human skeleton and two skulls believed to be more than 100 years old. The first skull was taken out at 10 o'clock this morning by Herbert Burger, a laborer. The stroke of a pickaxe shattered the brittle bones into small bits. An hour later another crumbled skull was found and shortly before 2 o'clock this afternoon a complete skeleton was located. Efforts were made to take the skeleton out intact, but in attempting to pull the bones from the earth the brittle skull, ribs and leg bones broke into hundreds of pieces. This skeleton was lying on the right side, as though tossed hurriedly into the deep grave. There were no indications of decayed wood to show that it had been encased in a coffin."*

People believed that the human remains must be the remnants of the bloody past that haunted Cayuga Street. All, or at least most, of the hauntings were connected to one building...the Columbia Inn. The inn had been built in 1815, one hundred years earlier, at the corner of State and Cayuga Streets. Over the years it became a popular gathering place for people in the area, including Guy Clark. Clark was a reputed abusive drunk and one night in 1831, he and his wife came into the Columbia Inn to enjoy a few drinks. During the night, Guy suddenly pulled out an axe and without so much as a word, he butchered Fanny with it. Clark was convicted for his wife's murder and sentenced to be hanged, the first man executed in Western New York. On February 2, 1832, he was hung on the grounds of the current Fall Creek School and buried on the spot while his body was still warm.

People stopped going to the Columbia Inn after Fanny's murder. William Brundage, the owner of the inn, realized that it would never recover from the bad publicity that it had gotten and closed it down. He had the building dismantled, and the lumber sold for new construction projects. A large portion of the lumber was used to build Carson's Tavern, across the street from where the Columbia Inn once stood.

Within ten years, a violent tragedy struck Carson's Tavern. John Jones and John Graham were having a few drinks together. There was no doubt that they were more than a little drunk when they left the tavern at the end of the night. The two men walked out the door together, though only one of them would make it home. Soon after leaving Carson's Tavern, Graham pulled out a knife, murdered Jones and threw his corpse in Enfield Gorge. Graham was convicted of the murder and hanged until dead.

With two horrific murders within a decade, people thought that the crimes were not a coincidence and looked for a common denominator. It did not take long for them to find one and they began to believe that the lumber from the Columbia Inn was cursed with something that could only be described as pure evil. Many in the neighborhood would not walk past the tavern and crossed the street before they reached it. Others changed their route completely, even if it meant that they had to take a street that was out of their way. Needless to say, no one shed a tear when it was reduced to ashes in an 1845 fire that started in the nearby Franklin House stables. The fire destroyed an entire city block.

Other ghost stories could be related to the acts of a more deviant criminal.

Edward Rulloff was born in New Brunswick, Canada to German immigrants. His life of crime began at an early age. After he served two years in a Canadian jail for embezzlement, he left the country and settled in Ithaca in 1841 where he took a job as a schoolteacher. He fell in love with Harriet, one of his students and they would eventually marry. Rulloff was a man with a mysterious life, and the mystery surrounding it deepened in June 1845, when his wife and infant were last seen. After intense questioning about the whereabouts of his family, he confessed to murdering them both. He claimed to have incapacitated Harriet with chloroform before slicing her throat. He then smothered the child and stuffed both of their bodies into a trunk which he threw into Cayuga Lake. Even though Rulloff had confessed to the murders, the bodies were never found, and he would serve a light sentence at Auburn State Prison for abduction.

Trouble seemed to follow Rulloff everywhere that he went. After he was released from Auburn Prison, he was convicted of the murder of his sister-in-law and niece and sentenced to Sing Sing. Finally, his reign of terror would end when he was tried, convicted, and executed in 1871 for the murders of two clerks in Binghamton.

Edward Rulloff was executed for the murder of his sister-in-law and niece in 1871. But did he also kill his wife and child 26 years earlier?

As Rulloff stood on the gallows before a growing crowd of spectators, he told the hangman to "Hurry up! I want to be in Hell in time for dinner." He also promised to come back and haunt Cayuga Street. After his body stopped swinging at the end of the noose, a death mask was made, and his brain removed to be studied. Could the skeleton or skulls found at the excavation site be those of his wife and daughter, or do they really rest at the bottom of the lake?

Duty, Honor, and Country

As the world was about to enter the twentieth century, the United States miliary was pulled in different directions. The Spanish-American War boiled in the Atlantic, the Philippine-American War raged in the Pacific. Asia saw political unrest and the nations of Europe began to grow restless. As tensions mounted, there was a heavy push to get the men in America to enlist in the military and perform their patriotic duties.

Armories were built in communities across the country. The large and cavernous stone structure at 900 East Main Street was built in 1905 to be used by the United States Army and New York State National Guard as a mustering point and training facility for new recruits. It was often the last place a soldier saw before going off to war, many of the men would never set foot on American soil again.

The Main Street Armory

Though the armory was built by the military, it was also used for other purposes. During the Spanish Flu epidemic in the 1910s, the armory housed and triaged thousands of sick Rochesterians. The hospitals throughout the city were overcrowded, doctors and nurses were in short supply. A skeleton crew of medical professionals did their best to care for those stricken with the influenza. Unfortunately, as with cities all over the world, many of the inflicted did not survive. Their bodies were stored in the basement morgue until they were claimed for burial.

At the conclusion of World War I the Main Street Armory saw little military action and community events flooded onto the indoor parade grounds. High school and college basketball games, circuses, and automobile shows were held there until the War Memorial opened in the 1950s. The Rochester Centrals, a semi-professional basketball team, played there from 1925-193, as well as the Rochester Iroquois indoor lacrosse team in the 1930s. The Iroquois most famous player was Jay Silverheels, who played Tonto on the popular 1950s television series The Lone Ranger.

The National Guard continued to use the building until 1995, after which it sat empty for ten years until it was bought at auction for $1000 by Scott Donaldson. He immediately began rehabilitating the armory, which was no small task for a man that was legally blind. Today it used for concerts and conventions.

After the crowds go home, strange, and unexplained events occur. There is paranormal activity on every level of this dark fortress. During its use by the military, the basement saw the most actions. It housed the indoor firing range, morgue, and military prison. The practice field had been converted into a paintball course and the firing range was silenced a long time ago. The spirits of the soldiers of the past are unaware of changes. The dark silence is often shattered by the sound of phantom gunshots. The cells of the makeshift prison have held many "guests" that are guarded by the spectral sentries.

The grand parade ground inside the monstrous building had seen thousands of people at hundreds of events throughout its 117-year history. But perhaps the most solemn and important role was one that it played during a time of war. When a soldier was killed in the line of duty, their flag draped coffin was ceremoniously returned to their home soil. Their remains were taken to the local armory until the family could arrange for their military funeral. Tradition was to honor the fallen and a soldier in full military dress kept a twenty-four-hour vigil, stoically and at attention, standing beside the casket. Though the armory has not been used for this purpose in decades, sometimes in the quiet of the night, this scene is played out again and again.

Equality - the Soul of Liberty

The Seward House was built in 1817 on a triangular tract of land in the heart of Auburn, New York by Elijah Miller who was charged with overseeing the construction of the Auburn State Prison. At least one mantlepiece inside the beautiful brick home was handcrafted by a sixteen-year-old journeyman named Brigham Young, the future leader of the Mormon Church.

The Seward House in Auburn, New York

William Henry Seward, the future owner of the house and staunch abolitionist, was born in the Hudson Valley sixteen years before the house was built. At the turn of the 19th century slavery was common in all the states. However, between 1797 and 1827, it was slowly abolished, at least in the Northern states. Even as a young boy, William saw the inequality and struggles of the slaves and as well as the freed men of color. He preferred the company of the kitchen slaves to the aristocrats that frequented his father's parlor. So it was at this tender age that he formed his view on slavery, which became a philosophy and belief that would shape the man that he would become.

Education was very important to his parents, though for him he could take it or leave it. But to appease his parents, Seward enrolled in Union College in Schenectady after he finished secondary school. Seward may not have had an interest in his studies, he did make sure that he was dressed in the highest of fashion. Being a "slave to fashion" had its downfall, Seward fell deep into debt. He did not want his parents to know about the bills from a local tailor that hung over his head, and he looked for a solution on his own. Seward could see only one way out, he dropped out of college and took a position as a schoolteacher in Savannah, Georgia to earn money to pay his debt. When his father found out what Seward had done and where he was, he was furious, and his mother begged him to come home. Reluctantly, he came back to his parents' home and returned to college, from which he would graduate in 1820.

Although Seward's first job was as a schoolteacher, that was not his aspiration. He wanted to be a lawyer and was admitted to the bar in 1822. Seward was offered a junior partnership in Elijah Miller's law firm. This is where the paths of the Millers and William Henry Seward would merge.

Elijah Miller had a daughter named Frances, who was also a friend of Seward's sister. He and Frances saw sparks when they met each other. Instantly they fell in love and knew that they wanted to marry. Seward asked Elijah permission to marry his daughter, which he gave with one stipulation. Seward had to promise that he would never take his daughter away from him as long as Miller lived. After the wedding, William and Frances Seward moved into the beautiful brick home that Miller built in Auburn, a home that Seward would often call a prison. For twenty-seven years, Seward lived under his father-in-law's thumb.

With Frances' Quaker upbringing and William's philosophy about slavery, they made a perfect team of abolitionists. The Sewards opened their home to be used as a stop on the Underground Railroad. Runaway slaves were hidden in the basement and in a small room above woodshed at the back of the house. Harboring or helping a runaway slave was risky and illegal, but Seward used his influence to skirt the law. Through the years they became close friends with the infamous "conductor" on the railroad, Harriet Tubman. After the Civil War ended, the Sewards sold her a piece of land down the road from their house, she built a small house on it and lived out her final years there.

William Seward developed aspirations to become a politician and he was a gifted speaker, which would take him far in his career. He was quoted as saying, "I think it is wrong to hold men in bondage at any time and under any circumstances. I think it right and just, therefore, to abolish slavery." Seward jumped into politics at a time when the United States was in moral turmoil, and he knew how to use his anti-slavery and anti-masonic views to his advantage. He served as the governor of New York State from 1839-1843, during that time he was viewed as an enemy by the southern states. Seward would reject all requests from their state governments to have runaway slaves returned to their owners. When his term as governor was up, he served in the US Senate while being groomed for the presidency.

Harriet Tubman, one of the most famous and influential conductors on the Underground Railroad.

His supporters thought that he was guaranteed to be the Republican candidate on the 1860 presidential ticket, but newcomer Abraham Lincoln won the nomination instead. Seward befriended Lincoln and would become one of his closest confidants and his Secretary of State. Seward would use his influence with the president on some important historical acts and policies. He even helped Lincoln write the Emancipation Proclamation that was signed in 1862 during the Civil War. Seward did not minced words when it came to his views on slavery, that combined with his friendship with Lincoln, made him the target in a murderous plot.

The Civil War ended, and the North was victorious after General Robert E. Lee surrendered to General Ulysses S. Grant at Appomattox Courthouse in Virginia. There were a few that could not accept the defeat of the Confederacy and plotted revenge. A small group of conspirators believed that all Southerners wanted Lincoln dead, John Wilkes Booth and three others were ready to take matters into their own hands and set a plan into motion that would change history.

Lee's surrender lifted a monumental weight from the shoulders of Lincoln, the war had taken a toll on the president and aged him beyond his years. Just five days after the war victory was declared, the Lincolns planned to join another couple at Ford's Theatre to see the comedic play "My American Cousin". Although President Lincoln did not want to go out, it was the first time he and Mary had been able to enjoy a night together and she convinced her husband that the play would lighten his mood, which was something that he desperately needed. When the theatre announced that the President would be in attendance that night, Booth and his co-conspirators decided that it would afford them the perfect opportunity to execute what they believed were well-laid plans. There were three targets: President Lincoln, Vice President Andrew Jackson, and Secretary of State William Henry Seward.

While Booth shot Lincoln in the head with his Philadelphia derringer, Lewis Powell was at the door of Seward's Washington, D.C. home. Nine days prior, Seward had been seriously injured in a carriage accident and received a broken arm and fractured jaw. This would prove to be the perfect cover for Powell to gain access to the Secretary of State. When a servant answered the door, Powell told him that he had medicine for Seward that needed to be hand delivered to him and him only. As Powell made his way to the top of the stairs, he was confronted by William's son Frederick, who told Powell that his father was sleeping and was not to be disturbed. Powell turned as if to leave, grabbed a gun from the pocket of his coat, spun around and pulled the trigger. Fortunately for Frederick, the firing mechanism jammed. A struggle ensued and Powell struck Frederick in the head with the butt of the gun, leaving him crumpled on the floor with a fractured skull and his father vulnerable. Powell burst into Seward's room wielding a knife. He stabbed Seward in the face and neck and left him for dead. He survived the attack but bore the horrific scars for the rest of his life. The man who was to kill the vice president, got cold feet at the last moment and could not go through with the deed. The only fatality of the night was President Lincoln. He lingered for hours and died in the morning hours on April 15th, almost four years to the day that the opening shots of the Civil War were fired on Fort Sumter in the harbor of Charleston, South Carolina. The museum at the Seward House in Auburn has a piece of bloody cloth from the night shirt that Seward wore on that fateful night.

Frances was not with her husband in Washington, D.C., and although William would fully recover from his injuries, his wife never recovered from the mental scars that she suffered from the incident. She became a neurotic invalid and died from a massive heart attack not even two months later. William was devastated by her death. For two long years he mourned her death, but a light would come into his life.

He became enthralled with Olive Risley, a woman 44 years his junior and daughter of his longtime friend. Seward showered Olive with affection and favors, and they enjoyed their daily carriage ride. People were quick to notice the couple and rumors spread around town that they were going to marry. However, instead of dispelling the rumors, he created a scandal when his adopted Olive instead of marrying her.

At 68-year-old, Seward's health began to fail. Thinking a change of scenery would help, Olive accompanied him on a trip around the world. It seemed to work because when they returned, his health seemed to be renewed. But the effects did not last long and within three months is changed drastically for the worse. On October 10, 1872, while he worked in his library Seward grew short of breath. He lay on the couch and told his children to "love one another," after which he drew his last breath. The couch on which he slipped into the afterlife still sits in the library of the house.

The state and nation mourned the loss of William Henry Seward. This is a portion of his obituary that appeared in the New York Times – *A brief telegram announces the death of ex-governor William Seward, yesterday afternoon, at his residence in Auburn. The sad event was not wholly unexpected, as Mr. Seward had been in feeble health for some time. The decease of Mr. Seward removes another of those men who stood firm and steadfast in their loyalty to the Union in the days of darkest peril, when the tide of secession bade fair to destroy the nation and overthrow the work achieved by the Revolution and prosperity. The devoted group of patriotic men – Lincoln, Stanton, and Seward – have gone to their eternal rest, but pages of American history will forever be brighter and clearer for the deeds performed by them..."*

Secretary of State William Henry Seward

William Henry Seward was laid to rest in Fort Hill Cemetery beside his wife, two daughters and Elijah Miller. The cemetery had its own haunted history, but that is a story for another day. Forty-one years later, the Sewards' friend Harriet Tubman, would be buried in an adjacent plot, beside that man she called her brother.

The Seward House was a place that saw happy times, as well as turbulent times. Most of the ghost stories of the house as related to what was one of the darkest periods in our nation's history. The apparition of a short black woman with her faced covered has been seen on many occasions walking towards the house with a girl about fourteen years old. When the pair reach the door, they vanish as if they faded into the wood. Some believe that it is Harriet Tubman bringing a runaway slave to the safety of the Seward house, reliving an important and defining scene from its past.

Freedom and Hope

Esperanza Mansion sits on a hilltop in Bluff Point, near Penn Yan, with a commanding view of Keuka Lake. The mansion, and its estate, have a history that spans over two centuries. It all began in 1798 when John Beddoe came from Wales to the shores of the "crooked lake" and bought a beautiful tract of land. On the land, he built a small house in which his family grew and prospered.

Around the same times, over six hundred miles away, another part of its history began to take shape on a plantation in Stafford County, Virginia. John Nicholas Rose was born. Soon Rose and his destiny would meet at Esperanza.

John Rose and his brother Henry migrated to the Geneva area with their parents in 1804. The elder Roses built Rose Hill Manor on the eastern shore of Seneca Lake. John grew up as a gentleman farmer and received a great education from Union College in Schenectady. After graduation, he moved to Yates County and bought the prettiest piece of land in the area from Beddoe. In 1829 John Rose married Jane Eliza Macomb, niece of General Alexander Macomb, from New York City and brought her to Bluff Point. Together they began to build their home, Esperanza Mansion.

Modeled after a Virginia-style plantation with a captivating view of the lake, construction of Esperanza Mansion was completed in 1838. Though slave labor was used during the two-and half-year project, Rose gave all the slaves their freedom when it was finished. Staying true to his abolitionist values, Esperanza was one of the last stops on the Underground Railroad before the escaping slaves reached freedom in Canada. Rose farmed the land and raised Saxon sheep. Within twenty years, the estate employed coachmen, farm managers, and house servants, the size and caliber of the farm was unheard of at the time in the rural Finger Lakes region of New York. Esperanza also gained a reputation for the lavish parties and balls held there.

John Rose died on November 7, 1870. At the time of his death Esperanza had grown to more than 1,000 acres. He was laid to rest at Beddoe Cemetery in the woods near his beloved mansion. Jane

Eliza moved to Branchport, where she outlived her husband by twenty-one years. When she passed away in 1891, she was buried next to her beloved John.

Esperanza Mansion build in 1838 by John and Jane Rose.

Two years after John Rose passed away, the property was sold to George Clinton Snow who was a vineyardist from New Jersey. He cultivated grapes on the land of Esperanza for his grape juice company in Penn Yam.

The next owner of the estate, Wendell T. Bush, a financier from New York City, who used Esperanza as his summer home. At the opening of Penn Yan's Sampson Theatre in 1910, Bush presented the owners with a hand-painted stage curtain with a beautiful painting of Esperanza in the center. Not only did the Bush's support the arts, but Mrs. Bush was also involved with social causes at the time and started a Women's Suffrage Campaign in Yates County. A year later Bush sold Esperanza to Clinton Struble.

After forty-one years death would again visit Esperanza. Adam Fritz was an employee of Struble's, and he and his family lived on the grounds. In the winter of 1911, Fritz's stepdaughter slipped on a patch of ice outside of the Branchport schoolhouse and was carried home. Katherine was in excruciating pain from internal injuries she sustained in the fall and her liver was severely damaged. The fifteen-year-old died just days later.

After a fire ripped through and destroyed the Yates County poorhouse in 1920, a facility needed to be acquired, so the county approached Struble with a purchase offer for Esperanza. The necessary renovations were made, and the new poorhouse opened its doors. A great depression hit this country and the population at the poorhouse grew, and like other counties all over the United States a dark cloud fell over it. No records were kept, people just fought to exist. The county was unable to afford to operate the poorhouse. It closed its doors, the remaining "inmates" were moved to other facilities, and it sold at auction.

Garrett Bacorn had the winning bid, but he had no intention of farming the land or living in the mansion. For two decades it sat empty, beckoning vandals to come through its open doors and wreak havoc inside. When Betty Bader bought the estate in 1967, she had her work cut out for her to restore it. Bader wanted to turn the mansion into an art gallery that showcased local artists. Unfortunately, she died before the work could be completed. It was sold again...and again...and again. Rats and other vermin made the old mansion their home, the roof leaked, and it became a party spot for local teenagers. Bottles and cigarette butts littered the rich hardwood floors and spray paint "art" covered the walls. Not the artwork that Bader had hoped for.

Before long Esperanza Mansion had a hot date with the wrecking ball. But the Wegman family saw its potential and saved it. They bought the whole estate and restored the mansion to its 19th century splendor and turned it into a four-star bed and breakfast. In 1995, the mansion and its property were added to the National Register of Historic Places. Today Esperanza Mansion is an event facility.

Esperanza Mansion lives on today and its history shows its resilience. Over the years it was a plantation, private residence, Underground Railroad station, poorhouse, gallery, bed and breakfast, and event venue. With such a diverse history and scores of people passing over its threshold, it is no wonder a few of the spirits chose to stick around.

A couple dressed in elegant 19th century clothing have been seen seated at a table in one of the mansion's dining rooms, oblivious to the waitstaff buzzing around them. Perhaps it is John and Jane Rose enjoying the view that they had worked so hard for.

There have also been strange occurrences in the basement. One wall bears the outline of a woman. No paint can cover it, the outline always bleeds through. And when people walk near it, the outline turns green. To whom did this mysterious figure belong? In an alcove where a small gift shop once occupied, an apparition of a slave has been seen crouched hiding in the corner, no doubt on her journey to freedom.

There is one last ghost that roams the manicured grounds...a beautiful lady in white, her story and identity are a mystery. No mansion or castle would be complete without a resident lady in white.

Ghosts on the Village Square

The Genesee Country Village and Museum is a living history museum in the hamlet of Mumford that has over 60 buildings from all over New York state. Each building is filled with artifacts that were authentic to the 19th century. During the day, the museum's 700-acre complex offers hands-on experiences and programs to educate visitors about life in the 1800s. However, after the hustle and bustle of the crowds dies down and the volunteers leave for the day, activity of the paranormal kind manifests itself. Though all the buildings are unique in their history, a few stand out in a different way.

Near the baseball diamond at the back of the village, is an odd-shaped building, aptly named the "Octagon House." Corporal Erastus Hyde, from Friendship, served his country during the American Civil War. After the fight on the battlefield was done, he returned home to his wife Julia, and they began building their home. Like many soldiers returning home, Erastus needed to find his place in society. He started out as a farmer and partner in a mill that made shingles, but neither job suited him. Erastus reflected on his life and came to the realization that he wanted to be a homeopathic doctor. Julia was an accomplished musician as well as an ordained minister in the Methodist faith. They were also Spiritualists. At the time, Spiritualism was a common religion whose popularity did not begin to wane until the early 20th century. The Hyde's neighbors believed that there was a room in the Octagon House where they held seances to call the spirits of the dead and conversed with them. Erastus Hyde passed from this earthly realm on January 7, 1931, two days later Julia followed him into the afterlife.

Since their deaths, all kinds of strange phenomena have been reported in the Octagon House, everything from footsteps and voices to doors opening and closing on their own. Then there is the incident with the dog. A friendly dog, most likely a stray, used to hang around the museum. One day the dog wandered into the Octagon House and sniffed around the place like curious dogs do. Within minutes he hurried out the front door with his tail tucked between his legs. The dog refused to enter the house again, he would only sit in the front yard and bark. It is said that animals can sense spirits around them that humans cannot. Could he have encountered Erastus and Julia or one of the many spirits that they called out by candlelight?

The Hyde House was the home of Erastus and Julia Hyde in Friendship, NY.

Next to the Hyde House is the home of John D. Hamilton from the Southern Tier town of Campbell. Hamilton lived his life differently than the Hydes. He moved to Campbell in 1843 as a shoemaker. By the time he built his grand home in 1870, he owned many tanneries from Campbell to Pennsylvania. He was a wealthy and respected pillar of the community, whose life was without scandal. Unfortunately, when John Hamilton died in 1891, his story did too.

The Hamilton House was not thought to be haunted until it came to rest beside the Hyde House. Could Erastus and Julia have called on the spirits of the Hamilton's from beyond the veil? Do not be alarmed if you hear Grandma Hamilton laughing or the doorknobs rattle as you pass by.

Of all the buildings on the museum property, the Hosmer Inn, originally from nearby Caledonia, has the most colorful history and resident ghosts. The inn had been built as a log cabin around 1800 by Major Isaac Smith as the Forest Inn. It served as a stage stop on the Ontario and Genesee Turnpike, which is now Route 5.

Sylvester Hosmer fell in love with the Major's daughter, Laura Smith, and married her in 1809. He and his father-in-law became business partners and when Major Smith died in 1814, Sylvester took over the inn and renamed it the Hosmer Inn. Business was very good for the Hosmers, and they were able to remodel the building into a two-story frame inn.

The Hosmer Inn could be haunted by a War of 1812 soldier Murdered outside the tavern or even Sylvester Hosmer who lived there until his death in 1854.

One of the spirits attributed to the haunting of the Hosmer Inn could from an incident that occurred in 1814. In the early hours of the morning, Mrs. Hosmer heard a gunshot and sent Sylvester out to investigate. Not far from the door of the inn, he discovered the body of a soldier which he brought inside. There was no identification on him, so authorities had to do some early crime scene investigative work and soon discovered that the mysterious man was John Alexander. They then determined that the young man had been robbed of his military pay and killed. The authorities went to the military encampment the next morning to inform them of Alexander's death and discovered that one soldier in his troop was missing at roll call. A search party found him with a great deal of cash on his person and he was charged with the murder of John Alexander.

Alexander's body was buried at the site of his death and memorial rock was placed over his grave. For more that seventy years after his tragic death, a mysterious flower bloomed in conditions that no other flower could survive. Named the murder plant, it was believed that the young man had seeds in his pocket he carried from his home that grew. Just as mysteriously as the flower appeared, it disappeared – never to bloom again.

Alexander's spirit is just one that is associated with the Hosmer Inn. Sylvester Hosmer passed away on the spot of the inn in 1854. Footsteps have been heard walking on the second floor, as well as an apparition that is seen in the basement and woodshed. Could the ghost of John Alexander have taken residence there? Does the spirit of a wayward traveler continue to occupy his room on the second floor? Or is Hosmer going about his daily chores even in the afterlife?

Hell on Earth

Tensions between the Northern and Southern had been building for decades, all the way back to when the United States won its independence from England. The main reasons were deeply rooted in the controversial subject of slavery. First was the economic difference between the North and South. The northern states built their economy on industry and manufacturing, while the south depended on agricultural products and would be in jeopardy of economic collapse if slavery was abolished. Second was states' rights, the South believed that each state should have the final say in laws that effected their lives and economy. Third, the advancement of the abolition movement and the North's plan to force its ideals on the South. And finally, the election of Abraham Lincoln was seen as a threat to the South's way of life and economy. The federal government wanted to take control and abolish slavery in every state of the union. Lincoln openly stated his opinion about its moral wrongs and how it went against the very foundation of the US Constitution that this country was built on. The South was convinced that if Lincoln were successful in his declaration that slavery should end in all the states, it would result in their financial ruin. His election to the highest office in the nation lit a fuse that led to the powder keg that would soon explode into a bloody war.

The feelings in the South were so heated that even before Lincoln was sworn in, seven states seceded from the Union to form the Confederate States of America. On December 20, 1860, South Carolina was first to secede from the union called the United States of America. After their secession federal troops refused to give up control of Fort Sumter in Charleston Harbor. US Major Robert Anderson claimed it for the federal government and Abraham Lincoln. For months, the South felt that Anderson's occupation of Fort Sumter was a slap in the face. The Confederate forces under the command of Brigadier General PGT Beauregard ordered his troops to begin the bombardment of the fort on April 12, 1861. For two days the fort was pummeled and when the smoke from the cannons finally cleared, the Confederate troops were declared the victors. These were the shots that started a civil war.

The next day Lincoln called for 75,000 volunteers to take up arms and fight to "preserve the Union." Across the North mustering points and camps popped up to train the thousands of new soldiers of the federal army. Camp Chemung in Elmira formed as a general recruitment depot in May 1861. The 30-acre Union installation turned out the "Southern Tier Rifles," a regiment that was 21,000 strong. Before they mustered out in June 1863, these men saw battle at 2nd Bull Run, South Mountain, Antietam, Fredericksburg, and Chancellorsville under the command of Henry C. Hoffman. As the war raged on, the number of eligible fighting men in the area had been depleted and the sounds of target practice was silenced. Camp Chemung was decommissioned until the summer of 1864.

No one thought that the "War Between the States" would last as long as it did, in fact both sides believed it could be won in a matter of months. Camps that once trained men going off to war were needed to house prisoners captured on the battlefield. General Ulysses S. Grant was quoted as saying "The men might be better in Northern prisons than shooting our soldiers in the field." Camp Chemung was situated at the crossroads of the Erie Railroad and the Northern Central Railroad, which made it the perfect location for a prisoner of war camp. Prisoners could be brought in considerable numbers by way of train. The amount of land the camp occupied and that it had already been used for military purposes sealed its fate. Barracks No. 3 was converted into the Elmira prison camp, and officially opened its gate on July 6, 1864.

Hellmira, hell of earth for Confederate POWs.

At first conditions at the camp were decent; housing, food and medical care were adequate for the number of prisoners it held. It originally had thirty-five buildings that could accommodate up to 5,000 men. As the number of prisoners skyrocketed, men were forced to sleep in tents or out in the open when the buildings were at capacity. The weather in New York can be extremely cold and unpredictable for at least seven months and those men would have been lucky to have a blanket to keep them warm let alone any kind of structure to shield them from the elements. Hundreds of men died from exposure, those deaths were avoidable. Southern families sent clothing, blankets, and other personal supplies to their loved ones held at Elmira, but Colonel Hoffman's men burned most of the items. One prisoner from Tennessee wrote in a letter home that the camp was "an excellent summer prison for Southern soldiers, but an excellent place for them to find their graves in the winter."

For most of the year, the land that the camp was built on was well-drained. However, in the late winter or early spring, the Chemung River flooded its banks. River water poured into the barracks and inundated the tents outside which compounded the prisoners battle with frostbite and exposure. Not only did the prisoners have to deal with seasonal flooding, but they also had to contend with Foster's Pond. The one-acre pond was often used as a latrine and a garbage dump, which was unsanitary and attracted a large rat population. The rat infestation was viewed as a curse and a blessing. Yes, the rats spread disease throughout the camp, but they could also be used to supplement the prisoners' meager diets.

When the POW camp received its first prisoners, they were well-fed. Early records showed that their daily rations included fourteen ounces of bacon and beef, as well as bread, potatoes, rice, and beans. Once Colonel William Hoffman, the commissary general of prisoners, learned that the Union POWs were held in horrendous conditions and suffered cruel treatment in the Southern camps, he cut the Elmira prisoners' daily rations to just bread and water. Within twenty-four days, 1,800 prisoners suffered from scurvy. Once scurvy gripped the camp, dysentery, pneumonia, and smallpox followed. 1,264 prisoners died as a direct result of Hoffman's actions. They resorted to whatever was needed to fill their empty stomachs, even slaughtering a dog that had the misfortune of wandering into camp. It is important to remember that men starved to death at Elmira from spiteful actions of the Union officers in charge, not from a shortage of supplies.

Elmira soon earned the nickname "Hellmira," as it was the deadliest prison camp in the north. Its twenty-four percent death rate was only surpassed by that of Andersonville in the south. An average of eight Confederate prisoners died each day from malnutrition, exposure, disease, and lack of medical care. In one day, a staggering forty-three men succumbed to the conditions at Hellmira.

Although there were numerous reports of abuse at Hellmira at the hands of Union officers, there were just as many reports of the same war crimes at the Confederate camps in the South. Prisoners made claims that the guards beat them, stoned them, and pistol-whipped them for reasons unknown to them. There were other punishments the prisoners suffered for breaking even the most trivial camp rules. Barrel shirts and sweat boxes were the most humane of the punishments given out.

If a prisoner disobeyed an order, they were bucked or gagged. This meant that they were bound to a horizontal rack by the hands and legs. A wood block was placed in their mouth and tied around their head with a rope. The rope was often tightened to the point that the corners of the prisoner's mouth would split open and bleed. There was yet another punishment that was more painful. The thumbs of the prisoner were tied to a rope and then that rope was thrown over a tree branch. The prisoner was then raised up until their feet were just above the ground, putting his entire body weight on the two digits. They were cut down once the intense pain caused them to faint.

Claims of murder were made against Major Sanger, the chief surgeon at Hellmira. Sanger was a damn good surgeon, but his judgment was clouded by his hatred of the South. In the early days of the Civil War, Sanger traveled with the Union army and was injured during a battle at Port Hudson, Louisiana which resulted in the amputation of his left leg below the knee. The resentment he held was taken out on the prisoners brought to Camp Chemung. Walter D. Addison, a former prisoner and hospital orderly at the camp, testified that Major Sanger ordered Dr. Van Ness to administer a solution of arsenic to the sick prisoners, which killed them. While Sanger was on post at the camp, he stated in a letter written to Brigadier General John Hudson that he had murdered hundreds of helpless Confederates. His exact words read; "I now have charge of 10,000 rebels, a very worthy occupation for a patriot, particularly adapted to elevate himself in his own estimation, but I think that I have done my duty having relieved 386 of them of all earthy sorrows..." Sanger also bragged to other officers at the camp that he had killed more rebels than any Union soldier. There was no hard proof to back the claims and therefore Sanger was never held accountable. There are no records that chronicle the abuse inflicted by the guards or deaths of prisoners who were poisoned by Sanger. But why would they have documented that? A member of the southern miliary once said that when a soldier died in the field, it was war; but when he died in a POW camp, it was cold blooded murder.

Despite the disregard for the lives of the prisoner at the camp, one local man was responsible for the respectful burial of the dead. John W. Jones was born into slavery in 1817 on the Ellzey Plantation, just south of Leesburg, Virginia. The Ellzey family treated their slaves very well, but the matriarch was an elderly woman, and the younger generation did not approve of their light-handed treatment. On June 3, 1844, John "boarded" the Underground Railroad and began his month-long journey to freedom in the north. He was immediately welcomed into the Elmira community and became the sexton of the First Baptist Church. By 1859, John W. Jones ran the Underground Railroad line that went through Elmira.

In the early days of the pow camp, the dead were buried in mass graves, which held nine coffins each, between Foster's Pond and the Chemung River. To preserve their identity, a piece of paper was tucked into their armpit with their name, regiment, and date of death. When the Chemung River flooded, water seeped into the coffins and made those papers difficult to read. John, as the camp sexton, knew that the men, those who had fought to keep his race enslaved, deserved a better resting place than they had been given. He orchestrated the purchase of land that would become Woodlawn National Cemetery and began re-interring dead in the mass graves. Jones did his best to identify the men and have their remains moved to the cemetery. If those who were first placed in the mass graves and became the unknown were considered, the number of soldiers that died at Hellmira would raise to thirty-five percent, or close to 4,200 – in just the 359 days that the camp was in operation.

If it were not for Jones' meticulous recordkeeping, the graves of the fallen Confederates would not have been given headstones when the Civil War was over. In a strange twist of fate, one of the bodies that Jones had taken such good care of belonged to the son of the overseer from the Ellzey Plantation. A marker outside the cemetery reads "Confederate soldiers were buried here with kindness and respect by John W. Jones, a runaway slave. They have remained in this hallow ground by family choice because of the honorable way in which they were laid to rest by a caring man."

Given the sad and tormented history of the prisoner camp and the number of deaths the occurred there in such a brief time, it is not hard to believe that the former grounds of Camp Chemung, Woodlawn National Cemetery and even the home of John W. Jones are haunted. The most paranormal activity happens on the grounds itself. Near Foster's Pond, the apparition of a Confederate soldier dressed in full uniform walks near the tree line before disappearing into the woods. You can sense your every move watched by sunken dead eyes and feel the heaviness and sorrow as you walk on the land that over 10,000 prisoners were held so far from home during one of the bloodiest times in American history.

Here We Go Round the Torture Tree

Let me set the scene. It is 1779 at the height of the American Revolution and tensions across the land were running high. Indian raiding parties attacked unsuspecting settlers in the name of the British crown. General George Washington, infuriated by the unprovoked guerilla warfare against the settlers, sent orders to General John Sullivan to take his men and displace the tribes; destroy their crops, village, and food supplies in retaliation for the raids on the settlers.

A patriot scouting party near Groveland on September 13, 1779, saw four Indians on the wooded trail ahead of them and engaged fire. After the sound of exploding ammunition ceased and the smoke from the guns cleared, one Indian was dead. As Lt. Thomas Boyd and Sgt. Michael Parker led the group back to Sullivan's encampment, a guide warned Boyd that it was a trap as five more Indians appeared on the trail ahead of them. Failing to heed the guide's warning, Boyd chose to pursue the natives. General Sullivan's men quickly discovered they were outnumbered and began to fight for their lives. Somehow eight men managed to escape and return to the encampment. But fifteen laid dead and the rest of the scouting party, including Boyd and Parker, were taken prisoner, and held in the Indian village of Little Beard's Town, which is present day Cuylerville.

Joseph Brant, a British loyalist and Mohawk leader, met with the prisoners and interrogated them. He told them no harm would come to them if they answered his questions, but as soon as Brant got the information he wanted and left Little Beard's Town, Boyd and Parker knew that they would not leave the village alive. Brant's men killed them both. Parker's life was ended swiftly, beheaded with one blow of an ax. Boyd would face a more excruciating and gruesome death. They sliced open his abdomen, pulled his intestines out and used them to tie the lieutenant to a giant oak tree, which today is known as the Torture Tree. Then Boyd was forced to run around the tree until he fell dead. After his death, the natives mutilated his body; cut his ears and genitals off, as well as his nose which was placed in his mouth.

It was two days before a search party with General Sullivan's army found the desecrated corpses of Boyd and Parker. Graves were dug at the base the Torture Tree and they were buried with military honors. After the army laid Boyd and Parker to rest, they continued to Little Beard's Town and burned it to the ground.

Historic marker on the road to Cuylerville. It marks the location of the Torture Tree.

Grave robbers looted the graves of Thomas Boyd and Michael Parker in 1807. The settlers in the area reburied them and prayed over the graves that the soldiers would get peace. However, peace would not come for the pair. Boyd and Parker made the ultimate sacrifice and gave their lives for the freedom of their country, and it was decided in that Boyd and Parker deserved a hero's burial. Their bodies were exhumed and re-interred on Revolutionary Hill at Mt. Hope Cemetery in Rochester. Somewhere during the trip from Cuylerville to the graveside at the cemetery their remains were misplaced and not discovered for over two decades. It was not until 1865 that they were laid in the graves prepared for them 24 years earlier. This was not the last place they would be buried. The Daughters of the American Revolution purchased a plot of land in the early 1900s in Mt. Hope Cemetery which they named Patriot Hill. It was determined that Lieutenant Thomas Boyd and Sergeant

Michael Parker should be placed in that plot with the rest of Revolutionary War dead. This would be their final resting place.

Was Thomas Boyd's commission in General Sullivan's army and his ill-fated scouting expedition cursed from the start. It is believed that it might have been. As Boyd prepared to leave home at the beginning of the American Revolution, his pregnant lover said, in from of his superior officers, "If you go off without marrying me, I hope and pray to the great God in Heaven that will be tortured and cut to pieces by the savages." Boyd refused to make her an honest woman before he left. Could his death be the true depiction of the adage "Heaven has no rage, like love to hatred turned, nor Hell a fury like a woman scorned"?

Not only was the life of Thomas Boyd cursed, but there are also ghost stories attributed to both Boyd and Parker. The spirits of the two men seem to be restless, it is not hard to understand why knowing the terror they were subjected to in their final moments and the fact that their remains were moved countless times. Shadowy figures have been witnessed replaying the horrible events that took place around the mighty oak tree. Local ghost hunters steered clear of the area once the sun sets, not wanting to encounter the Indian spirits that whoop and shout or the spectral horses that gallop in the distance. The Torture Tree fell to the ground in 1999, 220 years after it witnessed that tragic day. When it fell, the paranormal activity seemed to be silenced. Or was it? Visit the Boyd and Parker Memorial on Route 20A in Cuylerville at dusk and see what memories are still carried on the wind.

House Built of Glass

At 39 West Genesee Street in Clyde, New York stands a three-story, forty-three room, 1858 mansion with a sorted history filled with murder and death, and lingering spirits.

Aaron Griswold was a prominent Clyde resident, a successful businessman, banker, and owner of the Clyde Hotel. He was also a charter member of the Griswold Lodge, a masonic lodge, which was formed in 1867. Most importantly, for the purpose of this book, he built a mansion on West Genesee Street not far from the Erie Canal. When construction was completed Aaron and his wife Hannah moved in. They lived happily in their home until Hannah died in the house in 1870. Devastated by his wife's death, Aaron could not bear to stay another night there without her and sold the property to Mary and Jarvis Smith.

The Erie Mansion in Clyde, New York.

Jarvis Smith was one of the best-known physicians in Wayne County. The couple began renovating the mansion for their family, which included their daughter Eugenia and Jarvis' father Chester. They also had a female servant and a male groom. On March 16, 1881, Eugenia married Charles Ely, who owned Clyde Glass Works, one of the biggest glass works in the world at the time. After the wedding, Eugenia and Charles moved into the Smith family home. They had a son named William, who went by the name Billy. Remember the name Billy Ely as there is scandal and tragedy tied to it.

There has been a long history of death associated with the Smith-Ely House. The first death that occurred within the four walls of the mansion was of course that of Hannah Griswold, before the Smith's took ownership. Over a nineteen-year period, six people would die and seven funerals be held, though rumor tells that the death toll could be even higher. Again, more about that is later to come.

Chester Smith, in 1892, was the first in the Smith family to die in the house. Less than a year later the funeral of Mabel Smith, Jarvis' niece from New York City, was held on March 16, 1893. The family would get a reprieve from the morbidity of death and mourning until 1902 when Jarvis was struck down by abdominal cancer at the age of seventy-three. He passed away in the house and was memorialized there as well. Before Eugenia could heal from the death of her father, Charles passed away in 1903 from Bright's Disease. Eugenia's mother Mary passed away in 1911 after a long illness. The passing of the Smith family matriarch was tragic and left just two family members remaining, Eugenia and William. The death of the latter would be the most dramatic.

William "Billy" Ely, playboy and serial killer?

William "Billy" Ely served his country well in the air corps during World War I. After he was discharged, he traveled and partied between New York City and Clyde, earning him the reputation of being a Broadway playboy. His death would be the most dramatic and sudden of all the death's the mansion had seen. William had always been a devoted son, especially when Eugenia was stricken to her sick bed. He took care of her and tended to her every need. As he reached to top of the stairs with his mother's evening meal, William suffered a massive heart attack and died instantly. His funeral was held at the mansion, and he was buried in a sealed vault, forever asleep in a brass and plate glass casket that fit the son of Clyde's king of glass.

Eugenia was the last remaining member of the family, and she too took her last breath inside the walls of the house. In 1934 she passed through the light and into the waiting arms of her loved ones. Or did she?

So far, the history of the Smith-Ely family has been fact, but like most well-to-do families, history tends to have little sparks of controversy sprinkled throughout. Now for the juicy legends and scandals.

As I alluded to earlier, both the Smith and Ely families had money. As well as having the mansion in Clyde, the Ely's had a "little" place in New York City that they used when they wanted to escape from their mundane life in the country. After returning from a trip to the "city," they made the gruesome discovery. The headless body of their cook was on the kitchen floor, her head was never found.

The next rumor that involves Billy Ely is even more disturbing. It is no secret that Billy was a playboy, a ladies' man and a bachelor about town. The dirty little secret is that the family tried to cover-up a scandal. The rumor was that Billy took secret the identity of a serial killer and that his killing ground was both New York City and Wayne County, though no bodies connected to Billy were ever found. Whether it is just a rumor or the truth, it adds to the mystery of the mansion.

The Ely family owned the house until 1950, after that it passed through several hands before it was purchased in 2008 by Mark Wright. In those 58 years, it was private residence, a home for veterans, and low-income housing, after which it was abandoned in 2006. The empty mansion drew the attention of drug addicts and teenagers, its slow deterioration gave the village no choice but to condemn it. When Wright saw it, he could see its potential through all the graffiti and years of neglect. During the painstaking renovations the mansions paranormal past began to show itself.

The current owner claims that the house is historically haunted.

People are not quick to say that the Smith-Ely House or Erie Mansion has ghosts, but it has been labeled as being "historically haunted." A former tenant of the apartment house said that on a couple different occasions she saw a woman in white ascending the grand staircase. Another woman reported that she saw a black woman glide through where the original kitchen would have been. Could it be the cook that was brutally murdered? During the extensive renovations, neighbors would often drop by and share their ghost stories. A common experience that they all shared was about the woman dressed in Victorian clothes, who paced at the front door with a lantern. But the most terrifying experience happened to one of the workmen. He never disclosed the details of the encounter, but it affected him in such a way that he refused work in the mansion alone. Could it have been the spectral sounds, disappearing tools or vanishing apparitions that spooked him? Find out for yourself if you are brave enough.

Is There a Doctor in the House

Dr. Andrew Oliver came to Penn Yan in 1818 from Londonderry, New Hampshire with his first wife Margaret, before the town was founded in 1833 by Abraham Wagener. Oliver's medical practice began in Giles Kinney's Tavern while his house was being built at 204 Main Street. When their house was finished, he began seeing his patients there. Andrew became a very successful doctor, and in 1823 he founded the Yates County Medical Society. He also rose to the rank of high priest in the Royal Arch Masons.

The couple had four children before Margaret passed away in 1829. Andrew made sure that all their children received a good education, including William who decided to follow in his father's footsteps. After graduating from Geneva Medical College, William met and fell in love with Harriet Jones. When they announced that they were to be married, Andrew had a beautiful brick home built as their wedding present in 1852, the house that would later become the Oliver House Museum. William began his medical career on the first floor of his new home. As we will soon see, medicine coursed through the veins of the Oliver men.

The Oliver House, built as a wedding gift for William And Harriet Oliver in 1852.

In 1853 Jennie, the first of William and Harriet's three children were born. She was followed by William Jr. and last came Carrie. William Jr. attended the Buffalo University of Medicine to become a third-generation doctor. He joined his father's practice in the Oliver house and served as a surgeon for the Northern Central Railroad.

All the children of William and Harriet lived out their lives in their childhood home, and never married. And all, but William Jr., died within the home's brick walls. William Sr. was the first to die in 1902. A year later, Harriet followed her husband into the light after a brief illness, most likely tuberculosis.

Dr. William Oliver Jr.

After William Oliver Jr. died in the Canandaigua Hospital from a long, but undisclosed illness, in 1915, the following headline and obituary appeared in Elmira's Star-Gazette on April 6, 1915. "*His Death Breaks Line. – (Penn Yan, April 6) Dr. William A. Oliver, long a prominent practicing physician here, died early this morning in Canandaigua at the age of 58 years. The remains will be brought here tonight for the funeral and burial. For three generations have the Olivers been physicians here, Dr. William A. Oliver being a son of the late Dr. William Oliver and grandson of Dr. Andrew F.*

Oliver, who formed the Yates Medical Association a century ago. Dr. William A. Oliver was born here and was graduated from Penn Yan Academy and the Buffalo Medical College. He had been surgeon for the Northern Central Railroad here for many years. Surviving are two sisters, Misses Jennie and Carrie Oliver, both of Penn Yan. No funeral arrangements have been made."

William's funeral was held in the Oliver House, and after he was laid to rest, just Jennie and Carrie were left in the big house. Carrie would spend Christmas 1933 alone, eight days after Jennie passed. She spent the next nine years as the last Oliver and with her death the legacy of this prominent family ended.

Carrie Oliver made sure that the Oliver House itself would live on. In her last will and testament, she gave the house to the village of Penn Yan to be used as a museum. Since 1948, the Yates County History Center has opened it up to the public as one of their three historic buildings.

There are four documented deaths in the Oliver House, all members of the Oliver family, plus the funeral of the William Jr. Death was no stranger to these brick walls. The volunteers at the museum will tell you that they have seen and heard many things throughout the years. Most of them agree that a shadowy figure walks up and down the stairway between the first and second floor. Could it be Harriet taking care of her family in the afterlife. Visitors have commented that they have experienced the sound of footsteps coming up behind them and soft whispers in their ear. Two questions come to mind. Who is trying to communicate with them? And if it is a member of the Oliver family, how do they feel about people coming in and out of their home?

Little Short of Madness

Today the Erie Canal is used as a thoroughfare for pleasure crafts, a far cry from the images of barges and packet boats filled with passengers and goods for market over a hundred years ago. In the early 1800s, the use of canals to promote economic growth was not a novel idea, countries around the world had been using them for centuries. American engineers and business investors wanted to put a different spin on an old idea and reinvent it, but it took time for the federal government and the citizens of New York State to warm up the idea of such an expensive and risky venture. The government of this young country was hesitant to start building a canal in what at the time was the wild frontier. DeWitt Clinton thought that the construction of a canal would be advantageous to the economy and expansion of the nation. At every avenue he was faced with opposition until he became governor of New York. He made the project a priority and was able to convince the state legislature to fund this "little" project. On July 4th, 1817, as the nation celebrated its 41st year of independence, the first shovel was put into the ground and construction started on what would often be called "Clinton's Ditch." Though there we more doubters that believers, by the time the canal was completed it was deemed as one of the greatest modern marvels of the 19th century. The Erie Canal spanned 363 miles, connecting Lake Erie to the Hudson River and revolutionized the shipping industry.

As work on the canal progressed, town and villages formed along the banks, eager to take advantage of the "money" that would soon float by. When it was finished in 1825, no one could've imagined how much traffic would travel up and down this historic waterway over the next 197 years.

Adams Basin was one of the villages established during the canal's construction. A small general store on the north bank of the canal was commissioned in 1825 to provide the services and needs of the canal workers and barge crews. In addition to a general store stocked with all the necessities they would need, there was a small set of living quarters on the second. Two years after the store was built, Marcus Adams from Bloomfield, NY bought the store. The second-floor apartment was too small for Adams' family, so he purchased a home on Canal Road, around the corner from the store. Adams noticed that his customers needed a place to unwind and have a few refreshments after a hard day's work and added a tavern to the general store. Marcus Adams, a shrewd and successful businessman, always looked for an opportunity. When the tracks for the Rochester, Lockport and Niagara Falls Railroad were laid on the south side of the canal in 1852, he petitioned for the ticket office to be put inside the inn and Adams became its first stationmaster.

The Adams Basin Inn at the end of the 19th century.

A shrewd businessman rarely earned a favorable reputation. After twenty-eight years, rumors spread among the canallers that a man could get more than a drink and broken-down horses at Adams establishment (wink). The village was called the "Horse Jockey Capitol" and there "a gang of worthless harpies make their entire business to trade in old broken-down horses of boatman." Adams kept a diary and often wrote in it that he hated the reputation that his tavern and the village of Adams Basin had gotten. It bothered him so much that he eventually decided to move his family to Suspension Bridge near Lewiston in Niagara County. When Marcus Adams died on August 8, 1868, his family was returned to Adams Basin where he was laid to rest in Locust Grove Cemetery with his family.

Adams sold his properties before he moved to New York State assemblyman James O. Pettingill, but he didn't hold onto them for long. When Patrick McNamara bought it, he added a dining room and ten guest rooms for travelers. The string of owners continued throughout the 19th century, including Joel Milliner.

Joel's father was Alexander Milliner, whose childhood home was the very home on Canal Road in which the Marcus Adams family had once lived. Alexander had quite an interesting story to tell. When he was 9 years old, Alexander Milliner became a drummer boy in General George Washington's private guard and was the inspiration for the famous painting "Spirit of '76." While at the Battle of Monmouth in New Jersey, he received a wound in his thigh from a musket ball and almost bled to death. Not only did he recover from his injury, but he would re-enlisted in the military. During the War of 1812, Alexander Milliner served aboard the U.S.S. Constitution for three years as a member of the United States Navy. When his military career was over, he settled down and raised a family with his wife Abagail Barton and lived a full life up until the day he died in 1865 at the age of 105. Milliner was one of oldest surviving veterans of the American Revolution. With all the pomp and circumstance befitting the amazing military career that he had, Milliner was laid to rest at Mount Hope Cemetery in Rochester, New York. As for Milliner's childhood home, it was demolished in 1952 and a historic sign was placed there.

Before Joel Milliner passed away, he sold it to William O. Marshall. He renamed the tavern the W.O. Marshall Hotel. Like Marcus Adams, Marshall wore many hats. He ran the general store, tavern, hotel, and ticket agent. As the railroad industry expanded, the New York Central Railroad used the rails as well and a ticket office for their express and freight trains was placed inside the Marshall Hotel. As with the history thus far of the Adams Basin Inn, Marshall did not own the inn for long when another family, the Ryan Family, took ownership and renamed it the Ryan House.

Transportation changed throughout the 19th century. As the railroad industry grew by leaps and bounds, traffic on the Erie Canal waned. And by the end of the 1800s, canalers only stopped at the Ryan House water their animals at the livery and have a few refreshments in the tavern. Even as commercia traffic on the canal decreased, the state of New York saw it still have some potential. In 1903 Governor Theodore Roosevelt ordered the canal be deepened and widened to accommodate larger vessels. It took several years for crews to reach Adams Basin. Michael Ryan had the buildings moved fifty feet from the bank to make room for the improvements.

The drawbridge over the Erie Canal in Adams Basin just outside the door of the inn.

When work on the canal was finished, the canal and the Ryan House were ready to reopen, filled with the hope of renewed prosperity. However, the exact opposite occurred. Within three years of the reopening of the Erie Canal, draft animals (horses, mules, and oxen) were banned from the canal's tow path, Michael Ryan's livery failed. Steam power was the only horsepower that the barges needed. On the heels of this financial blow, rumors began to circulate that prohibition laws were about to be passed in Washington, D.C. This would be a death sentence for the business of the already struggling tavern owner. The Ryan House closed to the public in 1916 and became the private home of Catherine Ryan.

The next chapter in the inn's history is surrounded by legend and mystery...somewhat. The following has been passed down for decades. On Thanksgiving morning 1922, Catherine Ryan was making a traditional holiday dinner for her family that would be arriving later in the day. When her family walked in the door, they found Catherine laying dead on the dining room floor. Dinner was still cooking on the stove and the place settings had been set on the dining room table. The family, being so distraught over her death, boarded up the house and left it just as they found it on that day. For more than forty years the Ryan House sat empty and fell into such a severe state of disrepair that it was called the "haunted house" by all the children in the neighborhood. Every town seems to have that house, sad and broken.

This, however, was just a legend. Catherine Ryan did indeed die in the house in 1922, but on September 9th, not Thanksgiving day. The house was neither boarded up or abandoned. Catherine's son Frances lived in the house until his death in 1972. For 43 years, he lived in just two rooms of the house as a recluse. No repairs were done on the house and over the years took on the appearance of the classic haunted houses in Hollywood films. One thing part of the legend was correct, the Ryan House was truly haunted.

When Frances Ryan passed away, Bud Nichols and his wife purchased the old home and took on the monumental task of restoring it to its former glory, with one unique addition. The main entrance from the 1842 Nathaniel Rochester house in Rochester was salvaged by Nichols and attached to the former Ryan House. The Nichols first ran a small antique store out of it, but later decided to use it for its original purpose and opened the Canalside Inn, which would later become the Adams Basin Inn run by the Haynes. Today, the Adams Basin Inn is a private residence.

The last few owners of the house took the historic buildings life story and preserved it for generations to come.

Now that the history of the house is all squared away, let's dive right into the good stuff (not that history isn't good)...the hauntings.

Thousands of canal workers and travelers walked across the threshold of the tavern, and each left a little piece of themselves behind. The image of a woman, perhaps Mary Adams, has been seen in the mirror hanging behind the tavern bar and items move on the table in the guest dining room. A psychic walked through the main floor and immediately picked up on the spirits of two people who had died there, the spirits of Catherine Ryan and her son Frances. The second floor of the Adams Basin Inn had rooms named after people associated with the inn's rich history. Alexander Milliner's ghost is often seen as it glides by the leaded glass windows in the room that bears his name. On occasion people staying at the inn have unexpectedly attended an elegant spectral Victorian party, where the men wore tailcoats, and the woman were dressed in beautiful gowns. Some of the ghosts have been identified, but there are others that roam the halls of this canal side tavern and inn in anonymity.

Poor Unfortunate Souls

In the late 18th century Western New York was a beautiful wilderness with very few settlements in the area. With the Seneca Indian tribes' main meeting grounds were just outside of present-day downtown Batavia, the settlers that did brave the wild frontier feared Indian attacks. When the American Revolution was won, territorial expansion of the new nation became top priority. True pioneers were brave enough to live in the wilderness that was full of "savages," with little or no protection from the government. The fertile land, temperate climate and the hope of new prosperity and freedom drew them further west, regardless of the dangers they may face. The Big Tree Treaty gave Indian land to the United States and sent the natives to live on reservations. After this the frontier opened and people flooded in.

Small towns dotted the countryside, with miles between them. For those without a horse, the stagecoach was the only transportation to the world outside of their communities. Near the corner of Raymond and Bethany Center Roads in Bethany, once stood a carriage house and tavern. In 1790 it served as a stage stop on the route between Batavia and Warsaw, and to points further east and west. Weary travelers were happy for the opportunity to stretch their legs and get a drink, while admiring the rolling green hills that surrounded them.

Genesee was Seneca for "beautiful valley" and the countryside of Genesee County was just that. When the county was established in 1802 it encompassed much of Western New York, until other counties were formed from it. When the immense frontier opened, settlers began to buy up land as fast as possible to set up their farms and businesses. It became clear that many had taken on a financial burden that they could not handle, and they eventually became unable to support themselves. This was a problem that plagued the entire state of New York and in 1824 the state legislation declared that each county would be required to build an almshouse, or poorhouse, to take care of the ever-growing number of paupers.

At that time the tavern was the most central location in Genesee County. The carriage house and 133 acres were purchased to become the Genesee County Almshouse. Once it was ready for occupation, the following advertisement was posted in the local papers.

Notice is hereby given that the Genesee County Poorhouse will be ready for the reception of paupers on the first day of January 1827... The overseers of the poor of several towns in the county of Genesee are requested, in all cases of removal of paupers to the county poorhouse, to send them with their clothing, bed, bedding, and such other articles belonging to the paupers as may be necessary and useful to them."

If a person was a habitual drunk, lunatic, pauper, state pauper (a poor person who was blind, lame, old or disabled) or a vagrant, they were sent to the poorhouse. Essentially, anyone that did not have the means to properly care for themselves was sent to the poorhouse. If a man died and left his wife and children with no viable means of support, his entire family would be sent to the county home. If an immigrant was unable to communicate with town officials due to a language barrier, they could be sent to the poorhouse as well.

When the doors first opened it took in just a few inmates, as they were to be called. However, within a year, the number of inmates grew to the point that expansion was necessary. A small cobblestone addition was built to house the insane and "naughty" paupers. This addition allowed the county to make extra money by taking in insane inmates from neighboring counties.

Life at the poorhouse was miserable and extremely hard on the inmates. They had been taken from their farms and homes into which they poured their own blood, sweat and tears. Then they were placed in an institution with people that they did not know and, in some instances, could not communicate with. Married couples were separated for the first time in their lives. Men slept on one floor, while the women and children were housed on another. It was not a free ride either, they had to earn their keep.

The county homes were meant to be completely self-sufficient. They grew their own food in the gardens and orchards on the property and slaughtered their own meat. Adjacent forested land was purchased to supply the home with all the wood it needed for cooking and heating. The men worked all day in the fields and took care of the animals. The women cooked, cleaned, and washed the laundry for the entire poorhouse. For seven months out of the year, the smaller children attended school that was taught on site. The older children were sold out as laborers at local farms and factories. Besides children being sold into bondage, the adults made extra money from the sale of things they made such as coffins. Of course, all this money went to the county to offset costs, giving the inmates no opportunity to life themselves out of this unfortunate situation.

Genesee County Poorhouse, today the Rolling Hills Asylum, in East Bethany, NY.

   No one could ever complain about being bored, and laziness was not tolerated. If an inmate was physically able to work, they were expected to. Provisions in the rules were made to address the issue of inmates that refused to work. Those who shirked their duties were treated horribly. If one preferred to sit on their butt all day, the keeper was more than happy to oblige. The offender would be put into solitary confinement and given only bread and water to eat. If they continued to be difficult, they would be strapped to a chair and wear a hood over their head until they were willing to work.
   This was a cakewalk compared to how the lunatic inmates were treated. Quickly there were more lunatics than the keepers could handle, and it became hard for them to guarantee the safety of the others from the more violent offenders. To make matter worse, the courts began sending the criminally insane to the poorhouses as well. To help alleviate the burden, those who were violent, criminally, or acutely insane were chained to the wall in their room. The others would be locked in their rooms at night, but free to roam around during the day. The overseers of the poor pleaded for the state to address the issue of safety for both the inmates and the insane. In 1887 New York State mandated some changes regarding the handling of insane inmates. The acutely insane were sent to the

Buffalo State Asylum, while the violent offenders were immediately transferred to Willard Asylum in Ovid.

Even though this safety issue was addressed, there were plenty of other areas of concern. What happened at the poorhouse, did not always stay in the poorhouse. This was not Vegas. Word got out to the community, and they were outraged by how the inmates were being treated. An 1883 inspection uncovered proof that the Genesee County poorhouse was a breeding ground for pestilence. That same year a group of concerned citizens formed the group called the Local Visiting Committee of the Genesee County Poorhouse State of New York. What a mouthful! The group made regular visits to the home every three to four months, to help bring changes that would improve the mental, moral, and physical morale of the inmates. The stigma placed on the status of being poor had changed over previous 75 years.

The Genesee County poorhouse continued to receive paupers and drunks until the 1940s. With the creation of social security and other state programs, county poorhouses across the state were no longer needed. Rather than let the massive building sit empty, it made the natural transition to a nursing home. A tuberculosis ward was added when the area was plagued with a growing number of cases. It remained in operation until 1974 when it closed its doors for good and all the patients were moved to other areas facilities.

For nearly twenty years all that gathered in the large dining hall was dust and decay. New life was breathed into the halls in 1992 when the Carriage Village opened and then the Rolling Hills County Mall. Former inmate rooms were rented to small shop owners from which to sell their treasures. When the owners were unable to make the mall work, it closed its doors in 2007. The building was sold again and opened as Rolling Hills Asylum in 2010 where the public can perform paranormal investigations.

The main kitchen in the basement had a place to butcher the meat and a large walk-in freezer to store it. The morgue was in the basement as well. The freezer doubled as storage for bodies in the winter when the ground was too frozen to dig graves. During the tuberculosis epidemic, patients were dying at an alarming rate. When the morgue had become full, the bodies were wheeled into the freezer while they awaited burial. On more than one occasion a person would not be fully dead when they were placed in the freezer and they spent their last moments locked in a cold, dark room surrounded by the dead.

Even though a doctor was employed at the poorhouse full-time, more than 1,700 inmates passed from this world over its 184-year history. There is a record of who died, when and under what circumstances, but there is not map detailing the burials in the cemetery that is on the property. If there was a formal one for its entire history. There rumors that bodies had been unceremoniously dumped in graves all around the building. Six headstones from the 1800s were found in the basement and have been added to a memorial garden for the deceased inmates at the Genesee County Park on Raymond Road.

Though there were records of deaths, very few of stories have been shared about the inmates. Occasionally an obituary would appear in a local newspaper. Phoebe White was one of the first to be taken into the poorhouse, at the age of nine in 1828. She was declared an "idiot" and legally blind at 49. After Phoebe entered the home, she never spent a single night away from it until her death on January 29, 1886. Betsy McCumber arrived at the age of twenty and was also declared an "idiot." During her stay, she bore a son named Austin. Betsy remained at the Genesee County Poorhouse until she passed on October 10, 1893.

Not all the deaths were from natural causes, at least two inmates met untimely deaths. Harrison Rofs committed suicide in September 1830 and Dan Mach was strangled to death on November 25, 1885. These were not by any stretch of the imagination the only murders and suicides that took place within those walls. And not all the spirits of the dead moved on from their place at the poorhouse.

Though most of the inmates that had lived in the county home have been long forgotten, one story has survived through the years. Roy was brought to the Genesee County Poorhouse when he was twelve years old. He was inflicted with gigantism which left him horribly disfigured and already seven feet tall. Roy was the son of a prominent banker in Rochester and due to his father's influential status in the community, it was feared that Roy's disability would cause great embarrassment to the family. The only viable solution was to remove him from the public eye. And Roy's family subscribed to the theory of "out of sight, out of mind," and they never saw him again. He adjusted well to his new surroundings. He had a love of opera music and listened to it in his room all day long. And most importantly the staff and other inmates loved Roy and called him their gentle giant. At the age of sixty-two, Roy died quietly at the home. His shadow has been seen on numerous occasions by former and present building owners, as well as paranormal enthusiasts. It is rumored that when classical music is played, his presence can be felt in the room.

George was a kindly old man and former caretaker at the poorhouse. Even after he had outlived his usefulness, he was allowed to remain living in his third-floor room with his most prized possession, his organ. In the last years of his life, he had a tracheotomy which left him with a raspy, seemingly grumpy voice. But that could not have been further from the truth, he was a gentle soul. Those who have been in the building at night report hearing a low growl coming from the area of his bead and the sound of organ music waft throughout the building.

Not all the spirits connected with the Genesee County Poorhouse are remembered with love. Emmie Althworth, known to the inmates and staff alike as Nurse Emmie, was feared by everyone. She hated her job and made it her mission in life to offer no compassion to the ill and infirmed. Rumors have even been spread that she was part of a coven of witches that practiced black magic in her third-floor room. In the past local witches have broken into the building to hold ceremonies in her room and connect with her spirit. Nurse Emmie's ghost has been known to push people down the stairs and pull their hair.

Strange things happen at the old Genesee County Poorhouse, very strange things, including doors opening and closing on their own accord, misty apparitions appearing in the hallway, as well as voices and screams coming from nowhere. It is haunted by the souls of hundreds who had lived and died there.

The Chamber of Justice

It took eight hard fought, bloody years for the colonists to win their independence from the British government during the American Revolution. Victory allowed them to forge a path into the vast wilderness, a new frontier. Even though the "Red Coats" had been defeated, the woods were not yet safe from the enemy. Before the citizens of a new country, could go west General George Washington sent Major General John Sullivan and his troops to clear them of renegade Indians that had sided with the British armies and massacred innocent settlers in the name of the crown. Washington wanted to not only make sure the "western" frontier was safe for the expanding nation, but he also needed to make a statement that the Americans were a force to be reckoned with.

The town of Canandaigua was founded in 1788 and then a year later, the county of Ontario. Even though the frontier had been made safe from the native Americans, within the settlements, a system of law and order needed to be set. The first of three courthouses in Ontario was constructed on the town square in Canandaigua. Later that year, one of the most important events in early New York State history took place.

Signing of the Pickering Treaty

On a chilly November day, the Pickering Treaty, or the Treaty of Canandaigua, was signed. It would guarantee peace between the six Iroquois Nations and the young United States government. At the signing, the Iroquois were represented by Corn Planter, Handsome Lake, Little Beard, and Red Jacket. Two months after the treaty was signed in Canandaigua, President George Washington made it official with his signature. 228 years later, the Treaty of Canandaigua remains active. The history making day was commemorated with a rock on the square.

Vintage postcard of the Ontario County Courthouse

Lawlessness in the 1790s was not much different than it is today. The first jury trial west of Albany was held in the Ontario County courthouse, a serious crime at the time...the theft of a cowbell. Not all the cases heard in the early days were so trivial. Around the turn of the 19th century, a case that could have ignited a powder keg was tried in front of a judge and jury. Stiff-Armed George was accused of killing John Hewitt on the front porch of his log cabin. George was a Seneca Indian and John was a settler. Stiff-Armed George needed a good defense, and the great orator Red Jacket took on the case. The evidence was so great against George that not even Red Jacket's smooth talking could sway the jury to find him not guilty. The sentence of death by hanging was handed down in April 1803, though the punishment would never be carried out. Even though there was a treaty of peace, peace was hugging a thin line. Governor Dewitt Clinton feared tribal protests and riots and pardoned George nine years later. The pardon had strings attached to it. In exchange for his life, George had to leave New York State for good. Stiff Armed-George lived out his life on the Allegheny Reservation in Pennsylvania.

This country was built on freedom, including religious freedom. Though it was supported in the Constitution, many did not accept it. A perfect example was the trial of Jemima Wilkinson. Jemima was born into a strict Quaker family in 1759. A severe illness left her bedridden and on death's door. Prospects of recovery were bleak. Her recovery was a miraculous one, after which she would introduce herself as the vessel for Jesus Christ, God, and the Holy Ghost. People believed that she had lost her mind. Jemima also denounced her old identity and started her own religion and became a "Publick Universal Friend." Her neighbors treated her as an outcast and Jemima thought that if she moved to Penn Yan she could start over and practice her faith with no prejudice. She was wrong.

James Parker, a "friend" of Jemima, fought with her and soon became one of her biggest adversaries. He brought the charge of blasphemy against her four times. She was able to escape trial the first three, but with the fourth, she found herself in the Ontario Courthouse in front of Judge Ambrose Spencer. After a quick trial and a not-guilty verdict, Judge Spencer asked Jemima Wilkinson to address the courtroom with a sermon. When she finished her speech, the judge gave the following remarks to those in the gallery. "We have heard good counsel and if we live in harmony and do what this woman has told us, we shall be sure to be good people and reach a final rest in Heaven."

Just thirty years after the courthouse was built, a new one was constructed to replace it. The first one wasn't demolished right away but was renamed the Star Building and served as a courthouse, post office and storehouse until it was finally torn down in 1899.

The second great hall of justice was built in 1824. It would witness one of the biggest scandals of the early 19th century, known as the "Morgan Affair." William Morgan did not have an easy life to say the least and it was about to get worse. When he was 45 years old, he took 16-year-old Lucinda as his bride. Three years after the wedding, Morgan moved his family to Canada to open a brewery. It was a risky move, especially since he had absolutely no experience in the business. Though it wasn't Morgan's inexperience that closed the brewery's doors, it was a fire that destroyed it and his dreams of success. Within two years, they returned to the United States and settled in Batavia, NY to begin a new chapter in his life.

William Morgan tried to join the York Rite Masonry lodge in Batavia to become a Freemason, but he was denied membership. However, the old saying goes "when one door closes, another one opens." In 1825, William was able to join the York Rite Lodge in LeRoy just east of Batavia. He assumed that because he was now a member of the LeRoy lodge, he would automatically be accepted in the new lodge forming in Batavia. His assumption was incorrect, and William was denied membership a for a second time. He believed that he was on a blacklist and decided to seek revenge on the entire organization, not just one lodge. William Morgan worked with newspaper publisher David Miller to write an expose that would reveal all the secrets of the Freemasons. A scandal of epic proportions exploded within a year.

A depiction of the abduction of William Morgan outside the courthouse in 1826.

In August 1826, charges were brought against Morgan, and he was arrested. A local tavern keeper, and friend of the Masons, in Batavia accused him of the theft of a cravat and tie. Local law enforcement took him to the jail in Canandaigua. Miller paid the fine and Morgan was set free. However, as soon as he released, he was arrested again. The charge this time was a debt of three dollars. Today debt impacts your credit score and keeps you from getting things that you want. But in the early 1800s, an unpaid debt was a serious crime. Morgan was sentence to debtor's prison and had to remain there until his debt was paid in full. Miller didn't come to Morgan's rescue this time. Another man who was said to be a "friend," though most likely a Mason, paid Morgan's debt and he was released from the Ontario County Jail. Morgan and his "friend" walked to a carriage that waited in front of the jail for them. He would be seen alive just one more time, at Fort Niagara on the shores of Lake Ontario near Lewiston.

Most people then, and now, believe that William Morgan was murdered by a group of Freemasons as punishment for his betrayal. There are a few that thought he fled to Canada to start a new life. A month after Morgan was released from jail, a body washed up on shore near the fort. It was badly decomposed, which made a positive identification impossible. Two grieving widows, including Lucinda Morgan, claimed the body to be that of their missing husband. The mystery surrounding the disappearance of William Morgan has never been solved.

The courthouse/jail where William Morgan spent his last days was converted into the town and city offices for Canandaigua in the mid-1800s. The third and final courthouse to be built on the square was constructed in 1858. The most notable cases and heart-wrenching scenes happened in this building. Susan B. Anthony's trial and the only two murder trials that ended in execution were held there.

Susan B. Anthony was one of the most famous and vocal figures in the women's suffrage movement. Her outspokenness and tenacity made her a thorn in the side of many of her adversaries. Anthony and sixteen other women illegally voted in the 1872 presidential election. However, only Anthony was charged and made an example of. Also charged, were the election officials that allowed the women to vote. Susan B. Anthony walked away with just a fine, but the election officials were fined and imprisoned. Anthony's supporters sent money to help paid for her legal fees. Those donations not only paid her fines and legal bill, but she used the rest of the money to pay the legal fees of the officials as well. Even after her arrest and trial, Anthony continued to fight for the right for women to vote. Fourteen years after her death, the hard-fought battle was won when the 19th Amendment was passed in 1920.

Courtroom where the trial of Susan B. Anthony took place.

The Finger Lakes region of Western New York played a huge role in the abolition movement with "Underground Railroad" stations dotting the countryside all the way to the shores of Lake Ontario, "Station Masters" worked under the cloak of darkness to move runaway slaves closer to the freedom they sought in Canada. Hundreds, if not thousands, of the railroad's "passengers" made it to freedom, however the "train" was derailed for a few. The courtrooms of the county courthouse in Canandaigua felt the lasting imprint of emotions when run-away slaves were returned to their furious owners.

With a combined history of nearly 230 years that were filled with both tragic and celebratory events, it is no surprise that some spirits maybe hanging around the city square today. Red Jacket's apparition has been seen wandering the lawn in front of the courthouse, obviously unhappy with the two losses he had suffered there: the loss of his native lands and the case of Stiff-Armed George. Inside the courthouse, the spirits run rampant. Workers refuse to work in the third-floor jury room for the simple reason that it is "creepy." One judge can agree with that assessment after he saw a blue mist change into human form and then disappear right before his eyes.

The Seven Christmas Spirits

Fifty-eight years ago, 134 Market Street in Palmyra looked very different that it does today. Instead of the 195-year-old Historic Palmyra Museum, three small bungalows sat on that lot. One of the bungalows was rented by Paul and Ruth "Anna" Breeden, as a home for their family which included their six children; Sharon, Susie, Samuel, Dennis, Mitchell, and Marion, who was nicknamed Eddie. The family kept to themselves, and the children were regarded by their neighbors as well-mannered and behaved. The only other thing that was known about them, was Paul was employed as a traveling salesman. In late 1964 he was in Chicago to make arrangements to relocate his family.

On December 21, 1964 the plans that Paul Breeden had made changed and the small close-knit community of Palmyra would never be the same. At two o'clock in the morning a fire started in the Breeden's bungalow. Before the firemen could arrive on scene, the house was engulfed in flames which then spread to the other bungalows near it. A crowd of people dressed in their night clothes gathered in the street and watched to fire in disbelief. Many of their eyes scanned the crowd for Anna and her children. Though they were not seen, the firemen and police believed (and hoped) the Breedens had escaped the inferno.

Image of the fire's destruction from the December 21, 1964 edition of the Democrat and Chronicle.

When the smoke cleared, there was nothing, but destruction and it was then that the fate of Anna and her six beautiful babies was known. The fire had turned the three little houses to ashes, all that stood was a solitary chimney. In what was left of the Breeden's basement was body of Anna who had tried to shield four her children, Sharon, Susie, Dennis, and Mitchell, from the flames. The last moments of her life must have been horrific as she tried to save four of her children and worry about the fate of the two that were missing. Where were Eddie and Samuel?

Fire officials hoped that the two boys were able to reach safety and could just be hiding somewhere. It started as a search and rescue mission, the December nights in Western New York were frigid and they would not last long in the cold. Fire Chief James O'Brien called all the men to the firehall and asked each of them if they would join the search for Eddie and Samuel Breeden. It was reported that "none refused, and none returned dry-eyed." The search did not last long. Only a few feet from Anna and their siblings, the boys were found under a mattress the next afternoon. In the initial search many had passed by the mattress and never noticed the boys hiding place. The intense heat of the fire had dehydrated their little bodies to the point that they had been mistaken for dolls.

After the remains had been recovered, the focus became what caused the fire. No explanation was found, but rumors began to fly. Paul Breeden was thought to be in Chicago the night of the fire, but several people claimed to have seen him in Palmyra hidden amongst the crowd. He watched the flames destroy his home and family. People whispered to each other that he set the fire to free himself from the burden that his family placed on his shoulders. Others were convinced that he had a mistress and wanted to start a new life. It was said that when he made a public appearance just after the fire, he became so distraught over the demise of his family that he had to be sedated. Was it grief that overwhelmed him, or the guilt of what he had done?

The community was devastated by the tragedy. Seven lives had been lost. Eleven people were left homeless. A memorial service was held at the Presbyterian Church on Main Street before their bodies were taken to Tennessee for burial.

When the fire investigation was closed, there were no solid evidence of the cause of the fire. That meant that there was no evidence that Paul Breeden had murdered his wife and children. As of this day, the cause remains a mystery. Paul passed away in March 2010, did he leave this worldly realm with a clear conscience?

Many of the paranormal experiences at the museum are attributed to the spirits of the children, especially of Eddie and Samuel. As with children of all ages, Christmas was their favorite time of year. Perhaps they are still filled with the childlike anticipation of Santa's visit. Bonnie Hays, the former director of the museum, took special care each year when she decorated for the holidays. There is a fireplace and mantle in the firemen-themed room on the first floor, on which six stockings are hung for each of the Breeden children. A feeling of excitement will fill the air was each is hung one by one.

Historic Palmyra Museum, moved here from William Street in 1972.

Visitors to the museum should not be surprised if a tiny hand should take hold of theirs as they browse through the exhibits. It is just one of the children walking beside them. The children's spirits have been known to move items or make noises as they roam the halls. And if the air is just right, the faint odor of smoke can be smelled.

The building that occupies the site of the tragic fire is the former St. James Hotel and Riffenberg Saloon, which was originally located on Williams Street. In 1972 the idea of urban renewal put many old buildings at risk. The St. James Hotel was about to fall victim to that ideal, but before its date with the wrecking ball, the building was saved. It was moved to Market Street to become the home of Historic Palmyra, the local historical society.

The St. James Hotel was built in 1826 with twenty-three rooms that offered respite for the weary travelers on the Erie Canal. Canal workers, travelers, transients, and those running from the law would stay a night or two under its roof. It was even rumored that a prostitute or two ran their business from the hotel. Thousands of people crossed its thresholds during the hotel and saloon's long history.

The front room was the hotel's original tavern, a place for travelers and Palmyrians to meet and unwind. After a few drinks, things would sometimes get a little crazy. There was at least one documented murder of a man stabbed to death at the bar. If you look closely at the hardwood floors, you will see the permanent groove worn into it by the constantly movement of the bartender, serving drinks to those who were bellied up to the bar.

The children are not the only spirits from the past that make their presence known. The sound of high heeled shoes can often be heard clicking on the front room hardwood floors before they walk up to the second floor to one of the rooms. Like most ghostly encounters, there was no one in the tavern and no one walked up the stairs. Could it be a Lady of the Night waiting on her John?

Being a museum, it is filled with artifacts that span a large historic timeline. It does not just chronicle the history of Palmyra, but that of our great nation as well. Each room on the second floor is themed, the Civil War room, medical room, mourning room, and religious room. As each room is unique in its content, each room is also unique in its ghost stories as well. A person can stand in the center of the medical room with their hand stretched out and an unexplained electric feeling will flow through it. Perhaps the people treated by the primitive antique medical devices left a little piece of their energy behind. The mannequin hand stored in the room down the halls has the habit of mysterious flight from the closet shelf it sits to the floor below. And musical instruments housed in the religious room play a little tune on their own.

Historic Palmyra is not just the former St. James Hotel; it consists of five buildings total. The other buildings that they maintain are the William Phelps General Store, print shop, tenant house and the Alling Coverlet Museum. The history and stories regarding the Williams Phelps General Store give rival to the St. James.

Known as The Phelps, it is a large brick building that was also constructed in 1826 at the start of the Erie Canal's reign through Western New York. It served the needs of the canalers and area residents as a boarding house, tavern, and bakery. The Phelps stood as an anchor on Palmyra's "bloody corners." When the canal opened, Palmyra was part of the wild west, the streets of the small port village more resembled those of Deadwood, South Dakota than the quiet Victorian town that it is today. Violence and mischief lurked behind every shadow. The original entrance to The Phelps faced the canal on the northside of the building. The 1826 door still hangs, covered with the dirty hand and boot prints, as well as the energy of 196 years.

William Phelps General Store as he left it in 1940.

Around 1870 William Phelps purchased the building as a business and home for his family. The second and third floors were remodeled as their home, which ended the building's career as a boarding house. As a general store, it was the same as the others at the time. Shelves lined the walls from floor to ceiling behind the elegant glass and wood counters. Fresh produce was placed in wicker and slat baskets that ran down the center of the store. An ornate cash register and scale graced the top of the counter. When visitors enter the store today, it is like they stepped through a time warp one hundred years in the past. William's son Julius locked the store door for the last time in 1940, leaving it suspended in time.

There is a large tin-shaded lamp that hangs from the ceiling in the center of the store that swings gently on its chain from time to time, as it set in motion by an unseen hand or perhaps an icy phantom breeze. What general store would be complete without a cat curled up in the window? Several museum volunteers have been stopped in their tracks as a spectral black cat walked in front of them.

There are two ways to get to the second floor. One is through the original 1826 door and down a dark corridor used for storage. There is a bathroom at the base of the stairs that young men are warned not to use. Sibyl Phelps, the daughter of Julius, likes to lock the door while men use the facilities, leaving them trapped until a passerby hears their cries for help.

The second floor itself has eight rooms, which includes the dining room, two sitting rooms, kitchen, sick room, and small vestibule where Sibyl practiced her piano. People that visit The Phelps have experienced unexplained phenomena in each room. The shadow of a small boy has been seen running through the kitchen before it disappears into a door which rattles when the shadow passes through.

The sick room off the kitchen has a grumpy spirit believed to be that of Julius Phelps. He spent the last days of his life in that room. His presence is subtly made known by a sense of heaviness in the air as he waits impatiently for the visitor to leave his room. He values his privacy in death as he did in life.

The dining room table is always set for tea and the lace curtain adds a certain touch of class to the well-appointed room. It was the proper place for women to meet over a cup of tea and share a little neighborhood gossip. People have reported that while they sat at the table, they heard the faint clinking of a spoon on the side of a delicate china teacup. Perhaps it is the lady of the house waiting for a juicy tidbit of gossip or news of a scandal in town. A cat can be felt curling around the leg of an unsuspecting visitor, though no cat lives in The Phelps. Many have the urge to reach down and stroke its soft fur, quickly realizing that there is nothing but air.

In the north sitting room there is the spirit of a little girl that has been named Holly, though it is unknown if that is her real name. She was not related to the Phelps family but came to be there by way of an accident. She was struck by a carriage on the street outside

The Phelps. Her battered body was carried into the sitting room while the doctor was called. She passed away before help could arrive. Next to the fireplace is a small table and with a variety of toys under it. Holly sits under the table and the toys are hers, gifts from visitors. Those who have sat on the stool at the table to talk to Holly are greeted by her holding their hand is if they are her friend.

The most prevalent stories about the Phelps family revolve around Sibyl, who was born as the only child to Julius Phelps and his wife on October 25, 1895. To say that she was different would be an understatement. She was a very talented musician and accomplished pianist, which got her into the first class of the Eastman School of Music, though she never graduated. Against her father's wishes, she dreamt of stardom and moved to New York City to follow her aspirations. People who met her, often said that she looked as if she had just walked out of a Jean Harlow film. When her money ran out, Julius refused to send her more and Sibyl was forced to return to Palmyra, heartbroken over the dreams she had not achieved. She gave piano lessons to kids in the village, while she immersed herself in a new interest – Spiritualism. Sibyl became a member of the Spiritualist church in 1926 and remained a faithful follower until her death in 1976. She never gave up her interest in theatre and entertainment and was in regular contact with circus performers that came to Rochester. Sibyl never married and after her father died, she lived her life as a recluse. Until the day she left this earth, the house had no electricity or running water. Her bathroom was the outhouse behind the store.

Sibyl spent much of her life within the confines of The Phelps and that is where her ghost is to roam. Her spirit has been seen walking through the kitchen or sitting at her beloved piano. In her bedroom on the third floor, an impression of a figure is often seen on the bed.

Although Sybil lived alone, she always loved a party and the attention. Every year around October 10th, a birthday party is held in her honor with members of the local Spiritualist church offering readings. Sibyl must approve of the festivities; her spirit makes frequent appearances at the bash.

Sybil Phelps

Where Water Falls

The story of Sweet Briar began over 2oo years ago with the sensational tale of its first owner, Horatio Jones. Since Jones' birth in 1763 at Downington, Pennsylvania, his life was an extraordinary adventure.

At a young age, as were many boys in the late-eighteenth century, Jones was a skilled rifleman. He joined the elite rifle company, the Bedford Rangers, when he was just sixteen years old and served with the rebelling colonists in the American Revolution under Captain John Boyd.

While on patrol in the spring 1779, the Bedford Rangers were ambushed by a party of Seneca Indians. Confusion and gun smoke filled the air, when it cleared about 30 men in Boyd's company that had survived the attack were taken to a village near Nunda where their captors tortured them. The men were forced to run the gauntlet, where men and boys from the village formed a line about 200 yards long and hit the captives with tomahawks, sticks, and rocks as they ran along the line. Jones ran the gauntlet first, he made it through without a scratch and the only man in his captured company to make it through alive. He earned the respect of the tribe and although his life was spared, he was not free to go. A woman in the village wanted to adopt Jones as her son because she had lost her's, but he resisted and tried to escape twice. Unable to navigate the immense dense ancient forest of Western New York Jones was soon captured. Eventually he accepted his fate and was given his Indian name, Handsome Boy. Over the next few years, Jones learned and mastered the languages of the Six Nations. He not only had to the respect of the Seneca, he would also gain the trust of their leaders and Red Jacket chose him to interpret his speeches.

At the age of 21, Horatio Jones became a man in the eyes of the tribe and was allowed to leave the village. He built a cabin, started to trap, and made his money selling the furs. A stranger stumbled upon his cabin; lost, hungry and in need of shelter. Jones welcomed him and shared the food he had with the man. The lost stranger turned out to be John Jacob Astor, a trader, who bought all of Jones furs and hired him harvest pelts exclusively for Astor pelts. Ironically, in 1906 the great-great-great grandson of Astor would buy the very land that had begun an empire.

General George Washington called on Jones to fill the post of United States Indian agent and he interpreted when the government dealt with the Iroquois. It was a post that he held for over four decades. At the signing of the Treaty of Big Tree in 1797, Jones along with Jasper Parrish, another former captive of the Seneca's, helped negotiate the terms of the treaty. The Treaty of Big Tree gave the United States government millions of acres of Indian-owned land west of the Genesee River and created ten small Indian reservations. For his work, Jones was paid the handsomely with 3,000 acres.

After the treaty was signed, Jones and his wife, Elizabeth, moved to the land given to him outside of Geneseo. He first called the farm they settled on Fall Brook. He would later establish Sweet Briar, named after the wild roses that grew there.

In his later years, Jones prospered as a farmer and was closely associated with the most influential people in the Genesee Valley countryside, while being able to keep true to the heritage of his adopted Seneca family. As is life, every incredible story must end, and Jones' final chapter closed on September 18, 1836.

Horatio and Elizabeth welcomed the birth of their daughter Julia in 1811. The same year that her father died, she married Benjamin Angel, a local lawyer who aspired political power, the couple remained at Sweet Briar. Julia supported her husband and after serving as the President of Geneseo, he because a diplomat to China, Hawaii and Sweden under Presidents Pierce and Buchanan's administrations, and travelled the world for eight years. When he came back to Sweet Briar, he once again dove into local politics, but after working for the federal government the political goals he had could not be found in Geneseo or Sweet Briar. When Julia passed on Christmas Day 1871, without hesitation Angel sold Sweet Briar to the Wadsworth family and left it all behind.

The Wadsworth family in turn sold the property to George Austen who was responsible for designing the grand home that stands there today. Financial and marital problems forced Sweet Briar to be sold at auction and the highest bid was placed by Major Winthrop Astor Chanler.

Winthrop was born in New York in 1863, the great-great-great grandson of John Jacob Astor, everything seemed to come full circle. He was a Spanish-American War hero and served as an aide to General Pershing in WWI.

Chanler devoted his time at Sweet Briar to fox hunting and horse breeding, the preferred hobby of the rich. He and friend WA Wadsworth were members of the Genesee Valley Hunt Club. After Wadsworth died in 1917 the group disbanded, later Chanler worked to revive it in 1922. To this day the Genesee Valley Hunt's tradition of their annual fox hunt is enjoyed.

At some point Horatio Jones' property was divided into two pieces; Fall Brook and Sweet Briar. Now that the story of Sweet Briar is known, it is time to move on the magnificent tale of Fall Brook. A gorgeous 90-waterfall inspired the name Jones gave his first farm. It is the ghost stories and legends that surround the waterfall which make it so magnificent.

Fall Brook in Geneseo, the site of an Indian massacre at the hands of General Sullivan after the American Revolution.

After the American Revolution ended, General John Sullivan cut a path of destruction through Indian villages that supported the British forces across New York State in retaliation for their brutal attacks on settlers during America's war for independence. Sullivan's army was particularly barbaric at Fall Brook. The legend that has been passed down through the generations is that Sullivan's troops forced a group of Indians from a local village over the edge of Fall Brook. The 90-foot fall onto the rocks below killed them all. Their doomed spirits were left behind for eternity to linger at the base of the falls.

In the years that followed, local settlers and Indians believed that an evil dwelled at Fall Brook. They were all afraid to go near the property after the evening shadows began to fall. All, except Horatio Jones who built a log cabin there for his growing family. The spot where Jones' cabin once stood has long been taken back by nature and is used for pastures and farmland. Many local believe that the ghosts of the area's brutal and bloody past are still staking their claim to the curse land.

Within These Walls

Eastman Colby, originally from Salisbury, New Hampshire, bought a piece of land from James Wadsworth in 1810 at 568 Colby Street. At the time Ogden was a vast wilderness and the Indians still hunted in the area which made the journey to Western New York from New Hampshire dangerous. If the threat of an Indian attached was not enough, the terrain could be deadly as well. A tree had fallen across the trail and blocked all traffic from passing through. While Colby tried to clear the way, his ax glanced off the log and severed his tibia just below his knee. He overcame the injury and was able to blaze a trail for families to follow their dreams in a new territory.

After the United States' victory in the American Revolution, our young country tried to build a relationship, though strained, with England. But as the frontier continued to expand, tensions once again began to boil, and England continued to encourage the Indians to attack the settlers. England and France were at war which hindered trade with France. President James Madison grew frustrated with England's behavior and started to call the state militias to arms with the anticipation that war with England would be inevitable. Eastman Colby was one of the men from Ogden that answered the call to arms and began to train at a local mustering point and soon the men were ready to fight.

On June 18, 1812, President Madison declared war against the British Crown. Colby served in a regiment lead by General Atchison and the men elected him to the rank of Colonel while in the field. The war lasted nearly three years and after it was over, the brave men of Ogden returned to their families and resumed their lives as farmers, laborers, and businessmen. Eastman Colby returned to his farm, and though his military career ended, he still loved to be called Colonel Colby.

Colby sold his house on Colby Street to fellow veteran Aaron Arnold. Arnold was quite the character, he had a nickname "Deacon Arnold," as he was the deacon at the local Presbyterian Church. While he was a religious man, he still enjoyed a nip or two (or three). Once he bought the farm, he built a still to make whiskey. From that still he supplied liquor to several of the families in the area, whatever whiskey was left Arnold took to Rochester in a small two-wheel cart.

Both Eastman Colby and Aaron Arnold died in 1859. Colby was laid to rest in the Colby Street Cemetery just down the road from his original homestead. When Arnold died, he left the farm to his two sons. Neither wanted it, so they sold the property to their sister and brother-in-law.

The Colby-Pulver House is the home of the Ogden Historical Society.

It is at this point that the property went through several hands. The farm was in the hands of Leander Danforth in 1868, who lived there with his wife and daughters, one named Florence. Florence married George Stamp and they had a son named Clarence. When Clarence was a boy, they lived in the old Colby house. As a young man, Clarence married Myrta French, and they had a daughter named Inez. The family moved from the old Colby homestead when she was three years old. And after Inez married Arthur Pulver in 1925, the couple moved back to her childhood home. Until 1966, members of the Pulver family lived in the house that is now known as the Colby-Pulver House. In 1966 Monroe County established Northampton Park, which included the original Eastman Colby homestead.

Today, the Colby-Pulver House houses the headquarters of the Ogden Historical Society and is open to visitors to walk through and see how the settlers in the 1800s lived.

The chain of ownership of the house may be known, however the history of what happened within its walls remains a mystery. It is rumored that masonic scrolls were buried deep in the stone walls of the fruit cellar. Volunteers have reported that when they are in the museum's basement, they feel eyes from an unseen source bore into their backs until they begin to ascend to the kitchen. Could the spirits be protecting a hidden secret? Many believe that the ghosts of Eastman Colby and Aaron Arnold still roam the rooms and halls of their old homestead, making their presence known. Footsteps heard on the stairs, breath felt on the back of necks and a gentle touch felt as if to say we are still hear and we are keeping watch.

www.ingramcontent.com/pod-product-compliance
Lightning Source LLC
LaVergne TN
LVHW012031060526
838201LV00061B/4558